What others are saying about
The Self-Publishing Manual

"Poynter is at his best when discussing such specifics as starting one's own publishing house; dealing with printers; establishing discount, credit, and return policies; promoting, advertising, and selling a book; and order fulfillment."
— *Publishers Weekly*

"As usual, our self-publishing guru, Dan Poynter, is on the cutting edge of the New Book Publishing Model. Volume II couldn't come at a better time...when we so desperately need it!"
--**Ellen Reid**, www.bookshepherding.com

"A deeply researched how-to book on writing, printing, publishing, promotion, marketing, and distribution of books."
— *The College Store Journal*

"Poynter covers the production basics but his emphasis is on the business of books."
— *Booklist*

"The strength of this book is the detailed discussion of various marketing methods."
— *Choice*

"The book is a must for those considering publishing as a business and, for writers who want to investigate self-publishing; it is eminently useful for its new and old ideas for those who have already begun to do it. A fine and handy guide by a fine and successful publisher."
— *Small Press Review*

"A handy, concise, and informative sourcebook....Expertly organized and chock full of hard facts, helpful hints, and pertinent illustrations....Recommended for all libraries."
— *The Southeastern Librarian*

The Self-Publishing Manual
The guide that has launched thousands of books

The Self-Publishing Manual

Volume II

**How to Write, Print, and Sell Your Own
Book Employing the Latest Technologies
and the Newest Techniques**

Dan Poynter

Para Publishing, Santa Barbara.

The Self-Publishing Manual, Vol. II

Para Publishing, http://ParaPublishing.com
P O Box 8206, Santa Barbara, CA 93118-8206 U.S.A.
Orders@ParaPublishing.com; +1-805-968-7277

Unattributed quotations are by Dan Poynter.

International Standard Book Numbers
Softcover   978-1-56860-146-5
Large Print 978-1-56860-147-2
eBook: 978-1-56860-148-9

Printed in the United States of America

Library of Congress Cataloging-in-Publication Data
Poynter, Dan.
Dan Poynter's self-publishing manual : Vol. 2 / by Dan Poynter. p. cm. Vol 2. of: Self-publishing manual. C.2009.
Includes bibliographical references and index.
ISBN: 978-1-56860-146-5 (trade pbk. : alk. paper)
1. Self-publishing—United States. I. Poynter, Dan. Self-publishing manual-2. II. Title. III. Title: Self-publishing manual, Vol 2.
Z285.5.P69 2009
070.5'93--dc22
2006010649 (Vol 1)

Mixed Sources
Product group from well-managed forests and other controlled sources
www.fsc.org Cert no. SW-COC-002283
© 1996 Forest Stewardship Council
FSC

Table of Contents

About the Author

Dan Poynter is a pioneer in book writing, producing, and promoting. An "early adopter," he is always on the leading edge of the industry. His *New Book Model* is revolutionizing the book industry and information dissemination.

Since 1969, Dan Poynter has written and published more than one hundred books including *Writing Nonfiction, The Self-Publishing Manual, The Skydiver's Handbook,* and *The Expert Witness Handbook*. He has also created more than fifty reports, nine audio CDs, four video programs, a dozen eBooks, and more than eight hundred magazine articles.

Dan not only works in the book publishing business, he studies the book publishing business. He doesn't just talk about book promotion, he teaches book promotion. He is a Certified Speaking Professional (CSP).

Dan Poynter's seminars have been featured on CNN, his books have been pictured in *The Wall Street Journal*, and his story has been told in *U.S. News & World Report*. The media come to Dan because he is the leading authority on book publishing.

Often described as "Mr. Publishing" or the "guru of self-publishing," Dan shows people how to make a difference while making a living. He has turned thousands of people into successful authors.

His mission is to see that people do not die with a book still inside them.

Acknowledgments

I have not attempted to cite in the text all the authorities and sources consulted in the preparation of this manual. To do so would require more space than is available. The list would include departments of various governments, libraries, industrial institutions, periodicals, and many individuals.

Scores of people contributed to this book. Information and illustrations have been supplied by Alan Canton, Denny Hatch, Dan Snow, John Harnish, Ed Rigsbee, Ellen Reid, Michael Russer, Michael Levin, Sam Horn; Pam Lontos, Joe Vitale; Patrick Ang; Dr. Mel Gill; Bill Frank; Gordon Burgett, Mike Shatzkin; John Culleton, Pete Masterson, Stacey Miller, Paul Krupin, Alex Carroll, Shel Horowitz, John Kremer, Brian Jud, Judith Briles, Morris Rosenthal, Maria Carlton, Val Waldeck, Mindy Gibbins-Klein, Joan Stewart, Rick Frishman, and many others.

Thanks to Arlene Prunkl for the editing and to Robert Howard for the cover.

A Word from the Author

These are exciting times in the Book Trade. Both entertainment (fiction) and information dissemination (nonfiction) are moving from the large, traditional publishers to self-publishers. Author-originated publishing is moving to the forefront.

For reasons of economics and speed, the world is moving from print to electronic information creation and dissemination. This book describes what is happening today and where we are going in publishing.

The Self-Publishing Manual has grown through more than fifteen revised editions since it debuted in 1979. This best-known, best-selling book in its field has turned millions of writers into published authors.

This book does not replace or supersede the information in *The Self-Publishing Manual*. That book describes a proven way to publish that is still entirely valid. The publishing and promoting sections are extremely valuable and apply to most books, both yesterday and in the future.

This new book carries the same well-known title with the addition of Volume II because it carries on where *The Self-Publishing Manual* (Volume I) leaves off. At Volume I's 480 pages, it is not economical to add more (expensive) pages to that first volume.

Welcome to exciting times in publishing.

— Dan Poynter, Santa Barbara, California.

Warning—Disclaimer

Chapter One

Book Publishing Challenges and Technological Solutions

This book explains how today's savvy authors are reaching their readers; it describes a new way to write, publish, distribute, and promote "books": printed books, eBooks, audiobooks, and others. This book is the heart of the modern publishing company's business plan.

- → Write about what you know and love
- → Print only the quantity needed (PQN)
- → Sell/Distribute your books electronically
- → Promote the book socially through the Internet

This is Virtual Book Publishing.

There is no single best (cookie cutter) publishing solution for everyone; you could be an exception to any method. Each type of author, book category, and author's mission are unique. This system works and is a great place to start; you will learn from it and evolve. This system is easy, inexpensive, and practical.

> There are several ways to publish a book. To find the best one for you and your book, get as much information as possible. Buy some books in your category and attend some seminars. They cost less than a mistake.

With new methods of book publishing, you can make more money selling your books for less. When information costs less, more people buy it. This system will make money for you.

This book does not suggest "publishing on the cheap." If, for example, you are considering publishing an eBook (only) to save production money, you may be disappointed with lack of sales. *Every* form of book has to be promoted; you must let your audience know each form in which the book exists. Book promotion will cost money and time—you must invest both of them.

This book is about how to use new digital technology and new ways to use the Internet to find and sell to willing customers. The publishing and promoting are less expensive because it is more effective for authors to get involved with publicizing their books as opposed to spending money on advertising.

Most of the books on book publishing and nearly all of the posts online are written by people with a   single publishing experience. While it is interesting to read a report of their journey, they are not sufficiently equipped to advise anyone on the best way to publish.

References. This book does not repeat information or resources available separately. This book refers to reports and other books for more detailed information.

In the interests of brevity and avoiding redundancy, this book will not rehash what has been said before. It provides the URLs so that you may read the original words rather than an interpretation of them.

One-third of all the books published in the world are sold in the U.S.; 47 percent are sold in the U.S., Canada, and the U.K. See (http://BookStatistics.com). Think globally. Via the Internet, people all over the world can find you and your book. You can make your book available to readers worldwide, but you should approach the easiest-to-reach, low-hanging fruit by pursuing these three national markets first.

Publishing virtually is especially valuable to authors and publishers living outside the US, Canada, and the UK. You can live in paradise and sell all over the world starting with these three large markets plus your own.

These are exciting times to be producing fiction (entertainment) and nonfiction (information) books. The ways of doing business are evolving.

pBook or eBook? Authors derive more recognition or "credit" for a printed book (pBook) than an electronic book (eBook).

AUTHORity ribbon inspired by Joe Vitale

A Virtual Book. *The Book Publishing Encyclopedia* is a "virtual book." It was written, produced, distributed, and promoted using the guidelines in this book. It is available as a softcover book, a LARGE print book, and an eBook (.LIT, PDF, MobiPocket, Palm, iPhone, eReader, and Kindle). Each is produced immediately when ordered; there is no inventory.

Therefore, the book you are reading is written from real-life experience.

Every book should go through four stages:

1. Creation. The book is written by one or more authors.

a) Most books are written by one author. Most good books are then cleaned up by an editor.

b) If you are writing with a co-author, see my book *Is There a Book Inside You? Writing Alone or with a Collaborator*. You will find the responsibility chart invaluable and the sample contract essential.

c) You can be the author without being the writer. If you do not have the time, skill, or inclination to write your book, you can hire a ghostwriter.

Contact several ghostwriters for interviews. Ask if he or she has worked on your subject matter in the past. You want a ghostwriter who likes your subject and who can bring additional information to the project.

For a list of ghosts and editors, most of whom also write anonymously, see http://parapublishing.com/sites/para/resources/supplier.c fm.

2. Production. The printed book must be designed, typeset, printed, and bound.

If you produce the pBook (printed) first, the file becomes the eBook. The eBook is already done.

If you produce the pBook first, you will have the script for the audiobook (aBook). Thus the aBook is nearly done as well.

It makes sense to pursue them all, but you should produce the printed book first. This is the most efficient method, and the one that will make you the most money.

If you sell out to a publisher, the publisher will have the book manufactured. If you decide to self-publish, you will work directly with an editor/book designer/typesetter (or use your MS Word file), cover artist, and book printer. *You* will be the publisher.

3. Distribution. Sending books to bookstores and other wholesale and retail dealers.

If you sell out to a publisher, they will handle the Book Trade. (Wholesalers and bookstores: chain stores, independent stores, and online stores.) If you publish yourself, you can reach the Book Trade through a book distributor. Either way, the playing field is level. You have the same access to the bookstores as a large publisher.

> Distribution gets your book into the stores. But it's up to you, the author, to get the buyers into the stores— to pull the books through the system.

Regardless of how you get into print, you will distribute to the nontraditional markets, also called "special sales." These dealers, outside the Book Trade, are often many times more numerous than bookstores, easier to reach, far more lucrative, and a whole lot more fun because you are selling into your own industry (your colleagues).

4. Promotion. Promoting your book is not mysterious and does not have to be expensive. It is simply a matter of letting interested people know you have completed a book they need and it is for sale.

Book promotion is up to the author. Publishers do not promote books. So do not think that even if you sell out to a large publisher they will handle the promotion of the book.

Whether you sell out to a large New York publisher or publish yourself, the author must do the promotion.

Celebrity authors such as Frank McCourt (*Angela's Ashes, Teacher Man*) spend months out of each year on the road making TV appearances, doing autographings in bookstores, and speaking at writers' conferences and other events. They are not at home writing all the time.

If like most writers, you are an introvert and would prefer not to make public appearances, see the easy, comfortable promotion alternatives later in this book. You can "promote" your book without leaving home.

Those are the four stages. When a book fails to sell, it is usually because it was not taken through all four stages. It was written, manufactured, perhaps distributed—and then the author became distracted. Or the author lacked persistence and failed to follow through. Sometimes the author starts writing another book, there might have been a family crisis, or the author did not realize who was responsible for promotion.

As you've seen, this book is laid out in the four stages: Writing, producing, distributing, and promoting. Each of the four sections or stages will then address the editions of printed books (pBooks), large PRINT books (lpBooks), electronic books (eBooks), and audiobooks (aBooks).

Changes in book publishing. The book industry has changed little since 1947. While technologies have improved, practices have not. Giving large book advances to a few celebrity authors, accepting returns from bookstores and adhering to three selling season per year have not made any business sense for years. The industry was ready for reorganization. The economic challenge of 2008-09 was only a stimulus that accelerated major change. The industry would have change eventually anyway.

> This downturn is different from previous ones, because it occurs at a time when publishers no longer have a monopoly, or even a strong grip, on the dissemination of information in society. Not with the Internet, YouTube, and social networking.
> --Michael Levin

The Apple iPod Touch and the Apple iPhone will all but destroy traditional publishing. It is already very sick. http://iphonetouch.blorge.com/2009/01/19/ipods-and-iphones-death-for-the-book-trade/

> A lot of headlines and blogs to the contrary, publishing isn't dying. But it is evolving, and so radically that we may hardly recognize it when it's done.
> --Lev Grossman in Time Magazine

The Death of Traditional Publishing
by Michael Levin, Michael@businessghost.com.

The publishing industry died last week. The economic meltdown was the meteorite that hit the dinosaur right in the forehead. The only surprise is that traditional publishing lasted this long.

The firings of industry leaders, mass layoffs at top publishers, and the decision of at least one other major publisher to cease accepting new book proposals for consideration, taken together, indicate the end of the influence of the major publishers. Sure, they'll be there to push celebrity books onto a celebrity-besotted public, through book outlets like Wal-Mart and your local supermarket. But the business that began with editors who loved books and published what they wanted is vanishing, a victim of its own inability to find a reason for being in the Internet and print-on-demand (POD) world.

The firings are an immediate result of the plunging economy, but the death of traditional publishing is really self-inflicted. Publishing became too big and too dumb to survive, a victim of its own arrogance and unfathomably foolish business practices. Let me explain.

Who chose this stuff?
Is there any other industry that chooses its newest offerings on the basis of the collective whim of a group of people (acquisitions editors) with practically no business experience? Is there any other industry that pushes out thousands of new products a year but offers marketing support to only a handful? Even the Big Three automakers, as dumb as they are, spend a billion dollars in first test-marketing and then promoting one new car with TV and other ads while launching it in showrooms. Not the new form of publishing.

Twenty years ago, publishers spoke of an eighty–twenty rule: 80 percent of the marketing dollars went to 20 percent of the books. Today, the rule is more like ninety–ten or even ninety-nine–one. If Dr. Phil is publishing a new book in the same catalog as a first-time author, Dr. Phil will get *all* of the marketing dollars and the new author will get crumbs. As a result, that new author's sales will be so poor that agents and publishers will make the (perhaps wrong-headed) decision that her Work is forever unsalable. And she'll never get another deal as long as she lives.

When I go to the library or the bookstore and study the new offerings from the major publishers, I find myself asking these three questions over and over again: 1) Why did they choose to publish this stuff? 2) Who do they think will really want to buy this stuff? And 3) What could they have rejected if this was the stuff they signed up?

After all, what are the major publishers giving us? Pretty much the same thing repeatedly. Political tracts that pander to the left or to the right (but offer much more heat than light). Diet and exercise books that rehash what every other diet and exercise book has ever said: eat less, move more. Motivational books that shamelessly re-cycle Tony Robbins, Earl Nightingale, and Napoleon Hill, either with a religious spin or a make-more-money-now angle, or a book whose authors have lots of speaking en-gagements and nothing new to say.

The CEO of a major publishing chain once admitted that only 2 percent of the books in his stores actually sell; the rest are "wallpaper." Who knew that major publishers are actually in the wallpaper business? They certainly don't act like they're in business at all, between the poor qual-ity of material they publish and the laughably feeble ef-forts they put into actually promoting and selling books.

ADD: Agent Distraction Disorder
And then there are the literary agents, as a class the least business-minded and least-organized people in the entire business world. If they worked in any other industry, their habits of letting projects languish, slip through cracks, and fall by the wayside would get them fired. Not in pub-lishing, the land without deadlines. I honestly don't un-derstand how most literary agents make a living. When it comes to staying on top of things, remaining in touch with their clients, and managing the book proposals they order up, they are notoriously irresponsible. I hear repeatedly, even from major celebrities who were solicited by top agents to become clients, "I can't get my agent to return my phone call or email." What are these agents actually doing? Maybe if they did a better job of screening projects and actually getting proposals for marketable, fresh books to publishers, the publishers would have more to work with. Or maybe not.

I call the approach of most literary agents to their work "ADD" for Agent Distraction Disorder. I don't know what's distracting them from doing their basic jobs—reading and critiquing proposals, and looking for deals. How most of them survive is a mystery to me.

Actually, it's about to become a mystery to them, too, because the future of royalty publishing is small advances or even no advances for all but a handful of books. Everything is moving toward a model where authors get a piece of the back end and not a generous upfront advance. The last time I checked, 15 percent of zero equals zero. So unless agents get a whole lot more efficient, they'll be looking for work in other fields, just like the editors who are losing their jobs.

So what's the future? There will always be millions available for the Hillary Rodham Clintons and other political heavyweights seeking book deals. Why? Because if you own a large publishing company, and you want to make a multi-million-dollar donation to a high-profile politician, you can disguise it as an advance from your publishing company. And there will always be room for what even the publishing industry used to call "non-book books"— stuff about cats, new diets, and new ways to find God without actually having to pray or do something for your fellow man.

The future is now—and it's all about you
So what's the future for the book industry? After a dozen years, the troglodytes who run the New York publishing empires have never figured out a way to survive in the digital era. The relevancy of major publishers today can be compared with that of the traditional music industry (all but dead), FM radio (all but dead), or the three major TV networks (still breathing, but of increasing irrelevance in a 600 channels/D.I.Y. world). The major publishers will still be there, in a humbled, slimmed-down fashion, but they won't matter nearly as much as they once did.

The future of publishing is in your hands, in my hands, and in the hands of anyone with a few hundred bucks to self-publish with a digital printing company or even to put up an eBook on their own website. In other words, the future of publishing is as much about narrowcasting as is music and video. You're the writer and the publisher (and the marketer as well). You get to choose your audience, you get to write directly to them, and you no longer need to grovel before literary agents and acquisitions editors at publishing houses whose jobs, quite frankly, are disappearing. Meet the new boss: it's you.

What do you with all that power? You sell like hell. You use the Internet 2.0—the social networking groups on the Internet—to come into contact with and reach the specific audience your book seeks. You connect with them through Facebook, YouTube, Twitter, GoogleAds, or whatever cool new thing gets released tomorrow. You put your ideas in your audience's hands (the same way new bands are independently putting their music into the ears of listeners worldwide), without the mediation of a jaded, over-commercialized publishing industry.

You get to say whatever you want to whomever you want—and you get to speak your piece right now, without waiting through the traditional two-year period when your ideas languish while you beg and plead for an agent to pay you some attention, seek a publishing deal, and ultimately have your book hang in limbo until it finally, finally reaches its pub date.

Your pub date is the minute you finish the manuscript, give or take the weeks necessary to run it through a typesetter and digital printing company or whomever you choose. This is unless you just decide to do the whole damned thing yourself, which is so easy that your ten-year-old can be your technical advisor, if you're too right-brained to RTFM (Read the f***ing manuscript). And a two-year wait will almost certainly place your book out-of-date. You want your completed book to be as current as possible, particularly if it is nonfiction.

It's exhilarating, it's fantastic, and it's here right now. Traditional publishing is dead, a victim of its own self-importance. Writers of the world, step over the carcasses of the troglodytes. A new world awaits, and it's all about you.

Michael Levin is a *New York Times* best-selling author, and the author of more than sixty books; he co-writes and ghostwrites nonfiction and fiction through his websites www.CelebrityGhost.com and www.BusinessGhost.com.

> We know the Book Trade is changing. Now we have to figure a way to monetize it; to get paid for our writing and publishing.

Vertical publishing

Self-publishing is particularly advantageous for new or fast-moving nonfiction. When you control the writing, manufacturing, distributing, and promoting, you can move faster. You can take advantage of new ideas, breaking news, changes in the book category, and changes in the audience, as well as other fast-moving windows.

> "Bookstores will die, old-fashioned publishers will die, and 90% of new books will be published by their authors as POD books and sold online."
> --Dan Snow, http://www.UnlimitedPublishing.com

Most books of the future will be quite different—and the future is now.

> **Web 2.0**, a phrase coined by O'Reilly Media in 2004, and refers to perceived second-generation of Web-based services—such as social media and Internet social networking sites (MySpace, Facebook, et al., wikis, communication tools (such as Twitter), photo-sharing sites such as Picasa and Flickr, and folksonomies, which emphasize online collaboration and sharing among users. For more information, check out all these sites on Wikipedia at

http://en.wikipedia.org/wiki/Web_2.0.
(A word of caution about Wikipedia: Information is updated constantly by any public users who choose to edit the information, so it is not always entirely accurate. Although it's a great source of information, you're best to check several sites to verify accuracy of information.)

Some nonfiction categories such as travel books will be replaced by wikis. A wiki is a page or collection of web pages created to enable people who access it to contribute or modify content. Wikis are often used to design collaborative websites and to power community websites. Travel wikis will be more specific and more up-to-date because they will be constantly updated in real time—contributed by travelers—people who have recently visited certain places.

Travel wikis will be accessible on PDAs and Smartphones; there will be no need to carry bulky paper books.

Books are further being "promoted" as authors contribute to social networks such as forums, listservs, chat rooms, and blogs. They are using their book as a credential and are exposing the title of their book with each post they make.

For an example/variation of this concept, see *Offbeat Guides* by David Sifry.
http://www.webware.com/8301-1_109-9956255-2.html?part=rss&tag=feed&subj=Webware.
and
http://u-publish.blogspot.com.

Web 3.0 is a term that has been coined to describe the evolution of Web usage and interaction that includes transforming the Web into a database. See http://en.wikipedia.org/wiki/Web_3.0. (Same caution about Wikipedia as above.)

Simultaneous publishing: the fastest, easiest, and most lucrative way to move from manuscript to book-shelf.

You can approach an agent, find a publisher, and self-publish all at the same time.

Simultaneous publishing is simply self-publishing first, and then offering printed books to selected agents and publishers. If an agent or publisher makes you an offer, you can run the numbers and make a business decision. It is okay to sell out if you're offered enough money.

The old-fashioned road to publication was to approach agents and publishers with a manuscript, query letter, or proposal. The response was to treat you like a common, amateur writer. On the other hand, if you send them an already printed book, they will be more likely to acknowledge you as a legitimate author. There is a huge perceptual difference between an unpublished manuscript and a published book.

By the way, both agents and publishers are very short on time. They spend only minutes, sometimes seconds, looking at manuscripts, proposals, and query letters. Most manuscripts end up on the "slush pile." If you get turned down, do not take it personally. A turndown is not a reflection on your writing or the book. It just means that particular agent or publisher didn't invest enough time to "get it."

It may be that you sent the query to the wrong agent or publisher. They specialize or have a track record in certain categories or genres of books. They simply may not have any understanding or interest in your particular category.

Nearly 400,000 titles are published every year; if all were placed on the bookshelf, that shelf would have to be four miles or 6.4 kilometers long.

The largest superstores have just 24 percent of the needed shelving. That's why every new book cannot be shelved in the stores.

> Old Publishing is stately, quality-controlled and relatively expensive. New Publishing is cheap, promiscuous and unconstrained by paper, money or institutional taste.
> --Lev Grossman in Time Magazine

Author–publishers should remember these guiding principles:

- Write what you know and sell to your friends (into your industry).
- Turn your passion center into your profit center.
- Maintain only a modest inventory.
- Bookstores are lousy places to sell books.
- Focus your promoting on your market with Internet social networking.
- Sell downloads whenever possible. Avoid carrying inventory.

For more frèe book-writing tips, see http://parapub.com/sites/para/information/writing.cfm.

Para Publishing
Where information and technology collide

Chapter Two

Stage One
Researching, Layout, Back Cover, and Writing Your Book.

While there are several choices when it comes to producing, distributing, and promoting your book, there is a single, new system for creating the product or writing it. Here is a way to save time by consolidating some of the writing steps.

Before you write another word, research your topic, lay out your book, and draft your back-cover sales copy. Your research will not only reveal the market demand for your book, but you will discover information you can use in your writing as well as valuable contacts for promoting the finished book. Compile this information in an organized binder. Read on.

Researching your topic

1. Make sure there is a market for what you are writing.
2. Gather material for your book.

> Research makes me learn.
> Writing makes me think.

Whether you are planning to find an agent, sell out to a publisher, or publish yourself, you need numbers. You, the publisher, need the reassurance of a definable, reachable market. Do this research *before* you write the book.

Sales figures. How can you get accurate sales figures for other published books? You really can't. Traditionally, publishers do not publish sales figures. In fact, they boast of the number of books "in print" (and waiting to be sold). The "in-print" figures show their commitment to the book—and often the number is inflated. Most books are printed in quantities of 5,000, but few of them sell through.

> If bookstores are returning books in great numbers, there's only one reason—it's because nobody wants them. So the publishers are mistakenly trying to figure out how to get people to buy more of what they don't want, instead of thinking through how to create and sell more of what people do want. Publishers do practically no marketing research before they buy a book.
> --Michael Levin

Nielsen's BookScan tries to count book sales. See http://www.BookScan.com/. They obtain purchasing information from a majority of the major retailers each week. In a typical week, sales of more than 300,000 different titles are collected, coded, and analyzed, producing market information for retailers, publishers, and the media. But they cover only 80 percent of the stores—just 4,500 book retailers—and many more books are sold outside these bookstores. BookScan is a subscription service. See http://www.slate.com/id/2142810/.

In order to qualify your project, you must get an idea of the numbers of prospective buyer/readers for it. You can't get *absolute* sales figures, but you can get *comparative* numbers. This exercise will not only help you to verify the need for your book, it will reveal the ways to find your potential buyers. Here are the steps.

A. Bookstores. Visit a couple of bookstores with a notepad. Large stores have a wider selection than small stores. Visit the right neighborhood. For example, downtown stores will have a greater selection of business books while stores in the suburbs will have more books on parenting and relationships. Some stores have special, enlarged departments for some genres or categories.

Look on that shelf where your book will be placed. Remember that your book will be compared (shopped) with the books adjacent to it. Look at each book. Think: if someone were to see a particular book on this shelf, would they also be interested in my book?

Chart the comparative books on your pad. Write down the title, subtitle, author, trim size (all measurements), page count, copyright date, edition, cover type (softcover?), ISBN, and price.

B. Online Stores. Log on to an Internet store such as Amazon.com. Search for your *category* of book and set the list for Publication-Date order. Now you will see all of the books in your field from the brand new ones and those going back twenty years. Chart the books that are close to your project. Write down the specs on your pad.

You will find many of the same books you found in the brick-and-mortar stores, but the ones in the stores are either newer or selling better. Amazon has infinite shelf space; room for nearly every book, good or bad.

At Amazon, the readers evaluate the books. Write down how many stars each book is averaging. Amazon also provides the sales ranks; it tells you how the books are selling against each other. Record the numbers.

You can research historical Amazon sales data by visiting http://www.titlez.com/welcome.aspx.

C. Ingram. Some 55 percent of the books sold in the U.S. move through the four Ingram warehouses.

Call the computer at Ingram at 615-213-6803. Follow the voice prompts and punch in the ISBN (found on the back) of any book. The recorded voice will tell you how many books are in each warehouse, what their weekly sales rates were, how many were sold last year, and how many were sold so far this year. Again, these are comparative sales figures. Write down these figures.

D. Magazines. How many periodicals serve the group you want to sell to? For a list of magazines and newsletters, see http://parapub.com/sites/para/resources/maillist.cfm. Click on "***Select a Mailing List***." Choose the categories for your book. If there are a great number of magazines for your audience, there certainly must be a lot of potential buyers for your book.

Go to the websites of the major magazines in your market, read editorial comments by the magazines' audiences, and look for the circulation figures. People who subscribe to magazines, do so voluntarily, and vote—subscribe—with their money.

Importantly, you will send review copies to many of these magazines and newsletters. Reviews are the least expensive and most effective promotion you can do for your book.

If you are a "participant"—active in your subject matter—you should already know the major associations and magazines that serve your book's category. For example, I am a skydiver and have been in the industry since 1962. I know nearly everyone, company, product, etc. in the industry.

E. Associations. How many clubs and associations have your potential buyers joined? What is the size of the membership of each organization? Do online searches and see directories such as the *Encyclopedia of Associations*, at: http://library.dialog.com/bluesheets/html/bl0114.html

and http://www.marketingsource.com/associations/.

F. Specialty stores. What kinds of stores do you antici-
pate your potential buyers frequent? For numbers of specialty stores and chain stores, see
http://www.vendorpro.com/stores.htm.

Of course, your book will be in bookstores, but you will
probably sell far more of your books through specialty
stores relating to your subject rather than general bookstores. See
http://parapub.com/sites/para/information/promote.cfm.

For other industry numbers, see
http://www.Ranks.com.

G. Events. Where do your potential buyers voluntarily
come together because they have a similar interest? What
events do they attend? How many events are there re-
gionally, nationally, and internationally? How many people
attend? Relevant conventions and other events are good
places to sell individual books and to make new dealers.

H. Catalogs. More than seven thousand catalogs are
published annually in the U.S.; 11.8 billion are mailed
each year. See
http://www.catalogs.google.com/.

You are not interested in "book" catalogs; instead, you
want specialty catalogs. For example, match a skydiving
book with parachute and aviation catalogs. How many
catalogs are there in your field? How many copies do they
distribute? Record the numbers. You will want to submit
your book to these catalogs; they will almost certainly be
interested in your book. See Document 625, *Selling Books
to catalogs* at
http://parapub.com/sites/para/resources/allproducts.cfm.

I. Google Print. You can research the texts of many new
books through Google's program. For information, see

http://www.print.google.com/. Search by title, author, or subject.

J. Statistics Bank. Fascinating numbers on book publishing:
http://parapub.com/sites/para/resources/statistics.cfm.

Whether you are selling out to a publisher or publishing yourself, you need numbers. Agents and publishers want figures; you need them too. If you are selling out, put these numbers in your proposal, your agent (if you have found a competent one) will think you are a marketing genius.

K. Newsfeeds. Have news on your selected news items sent to you. You can also use these sites to send review copies articles and news releases.
http://www.syndic8.com
http://www.NewsPad.com
http://www.moreover.com

L. Google Alerts. This is a modern clipping service. Google notifies you whenever your keywords show up anywhere online.

Go to http://www.google.com/alerts/
(Be precise in your keyboarding or you may land on a site masquerading as Google). Sign up and sign in.

List the keywords that interest you. List your name, your company name, your book's title and key category words. For my books, I list parachutes, skydiving, self-publishing, etc. There is no limit.

For multiple words, such as your own name, surround the keywords with quotation marks. E.g., "Dan Poynter"

You will be notified whenever anyone online mentions one of your keywords—so that you can respond. You can even choose which media you want monitored.

Types:
- ☒ News: Monitor all news as to what is going on. Get promotional leads.
- ☒ Blogs: Post to them.
- ☒ Groups, forums, chat rooms, listservs. Take part in discussions.
- ☒ Video: Post a comment.
- ☒ Web: What are other websites are saying on their sites?
- ☒ Comprehensive. (all of the above).

How Often? Once a day, once a week. You can be on digest, which daily sends up to thirty emails in one "digest," instead of one email at a time.

M. Twilert, This service has been described as a "Google Alert for Twitter." See:
http://www.Twilert.com.

N. Help A Reporter Out (HARO). Find out which subjects reporters and editors are writing about. They often lists their needs in HARO. You will be notified when a reporter is working on an article covering your subject area.
http://www.HelpAReporter.com

O. AuthorMapper. This is a free analytical online tool for discerning trends, patterns, and subject experts within scientific research. The service searches more than three million journal articles.
http://www.AuthorMapper.com

P. Category websites. Which and how many websites cater specifically to your potential audience? The more, the better. You will contribute to the sites and send review copies, articles and (positive) comments. Add these sites to your list.

Total up these entire Amazon, Ingram, catalog, and other numbers. Now you should have a good feel for what has been published in your area and what hasn't been done, what is selling and what is not selling, what your audience wants, how much you can charge for your book. These numbers will help you decide what to write, how many to print, where to make your book available and where to start your book promotion.

Narrow the focus of your book. Your research is likely to reveal a number of books on your topic. With more than 400,000 titles being published each year, the subject matter is becoming increasingly specific. Besides, readers want and need a book that solves a particular problem or treats a specific issue.

For example, as I have explained, I have technical books on parachutes for the manufacturers, designers, and technicians, popular books for beginning skydivers, booklets for those in the First Jump Course, lesson plans for instructors, and lesson plans for technicians. Each targets a specific audience.

Make your book more specific and you will sell more books as specific buyers identify with your book.

Lay out your book. Writing is just part of the assembly. Building your book is like building a speech with Power-Point slides. The computer simply provides you with more visual aids to help you get your points to your reader. Prepare a binder with each page looking exactly as it will in the completed book.

Traditional manuscript—just words on paper
Now, in addition to the printed word, you will add digital photos and scanned drawings to your manuscript as you write, pull information from the Web (yes, the world's largest library is on your desk), add resource URLs and hyperlinks to your text, search encyclopedias for background information, art sites for illustrations and quotation sites for quotations. You will draw from all these visual-aid sources as you draft the manuscript.

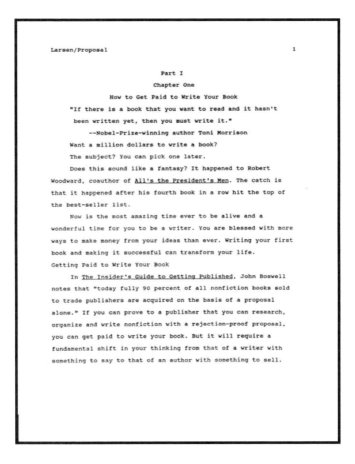

Traditional manuscript page

Traditionally, manuscripts consisted of double-spaced Courier type. Today, that format makes your Work look dated.

Make your manuscript look like a page out of a book. Set your margins so that the text block will be about 4.2" (106 mm) wide and about 7" (178 mm) tall.

Typefaces. MS-*Word* is not a typesetting program, but you can use its typefaces if you want to save money and

accelerate the project. For a better-looking result, you can deal with a book designer/typesetter who uses a page layout program such as *InDesign* or *Quark*. For a list of book typesetters, see
http://www.computorcompanion.com/LPMArticle.asp?ID=323
and
http://parapublishing.com/sites/para/resources/supplier.cfm
and
http://www.u-publish.com/design

For the text in a printed book, a serif typeface such as New Century Schoolbook (sometimes called Century or Schoolbook) is usually used. In print, a serif typeface is considered to be easier to read. Garamond is also a common font considered professional by book designers.

eBooks may look better on a screen in a sans serif typeface such as Verdana (like this book) or Tahoma. If you want fewer total pages, use a condensed typeface such as Arial (see the comparison, below.) Take a page of your Work, convert to each of these typefaces, print out the pages and compare.

If most of your books will be read on a screen, you may use a sans serif typeface for both the eBook and the pBook (printed edition).

This is Times New Roman, a serif typeface
This is Bookman, a serif typeface
This is New Century Schoolbook, a serif typeface
This is Arial, a sans serif typeface.
This is Tahoma, a sans serif typeface
This is Verdana, a sans serif typeface

All six of the above are 12-point typeface fonts. As you can see, the point size varies with the font.

To find the typefaces used in this book, see the Colophon in the Appendix.

Look at other books and see which typefaces you prefer. Certain kinds of books seem to look better with different typefaces.

Typeset as you write. To save time and to be able to visualize each printed page, write in page-layout format; not in the double-spaced, Courier typeface pictured above. Just set your margins, header, page numbers, type styles, chapter numbers, chapter titles, first paragraphs, etc., before you write a single word. Then fill in the pages.

To set your page margins in MS *Word*, click on *File>Page Setup* and change *top* to 1.8", *bottom* to 2.3", *left* to 2.5", *right* to 1.9" and *header* to 1.3".

For your text, select a typeface such as Verdana—this book's font—or New Century Schoolbook (sometimes called Schoolbook or Century) or, as mentioned earlier, Garamond (recommended by many book design professionals).

Once you've selected your font, click on *Format>Paragraph* and set the line spacing for *Single*.

If you can afford it, I strongly recommend engaging the services of a professional book designer to assist you with these issues of page layout.

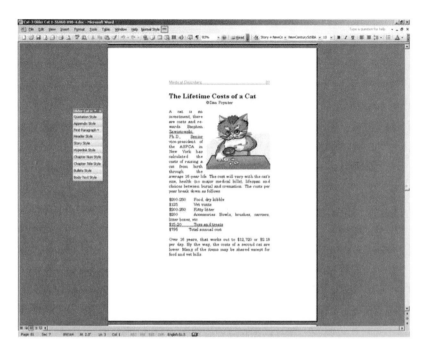

Set the margins, header, and page numbers

To make a header, with the book title and page number at the top of the page, click on *View>Header and Footer*. Type in the tentative title for your book, then click on the *insert page number* icon that is in the header and footer box. Underline both your header and your page number (as I have done above). Then set them in Arial or Tahoma, 10-point type.

If you have problems getting headers and footers right in *Word* it is probably because of the *Same as Previous* button being enabled. This article explains how to deal with the challenge: http://www.logicaltips.com/LPMArticle.asp?ID=356.

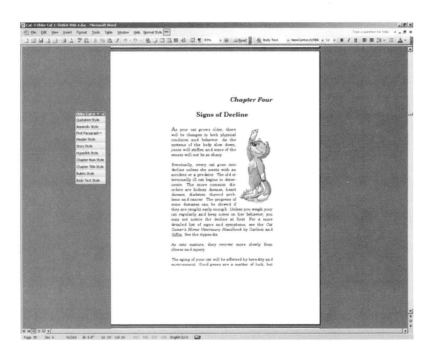

Position the chapter number and chapter title

When you write your book in book-layout format, you always know how many pages you have and you are trial-typesetting as you write. Now you are *building* your book; writing is just part of the assembly.

Writing your book is covered in detail in *Writing Nonfiction: Turning Thoughts into Books*. It goes into greater detail on how to break your book down into easy-to-approach bite like chunks (chapters), how to find time to write, assembling the binder (makes the job portable), where to find material (The Internet and peer reviews), and where to get illustrations, quotations, permissions, and stories to amplify your writing.

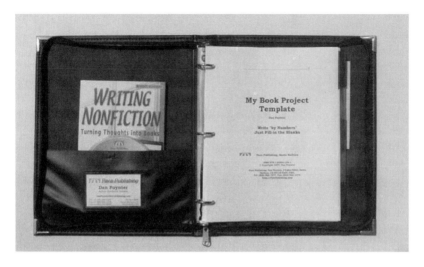

My Book Project. If you want more of the work done for you, see *My Book Project*, a book-writing template. *It consist of* a leatherette, zip-around binder containing a copy of *Writing Nonfiction*, a thirty-three-page book-writing template, and all the pages laid out on a CD so you do not even have to reproduce the outline.

Each page of the front matter (the ten or so informational pages prior to Chapter One, including CIP/copyright page, foreword, introduction, about the author page, table of contents, etc.), chapter headings and back matter (ap-pendix[es] index, colophon, order forms, etc.) tells you what to put on those pages. Thus, your book is structured and ready for your material. See http://parapublishing.com/sites/para/information/writing. cfm#mbp.

a) If you want to lay out the book yourself, use the mar-gin settings above.

b) If you want help with the layout structure, get a tem-plate for your book frèe from
P-47 WN Book Writing Layout Template. 34 pages, 373 Kb.

c) If you want the design and layout done for you, get *My Book Project*, described above.

Writing-by-numbers will accelerate your book development by helping you visualize the entire project and by guiding you through the writing process.

Draft the back cover before you write the book. One of the greatest obstacles to book writing is focus; lack of a center of attention. Before you write one word, get Document 116 (frèe) from http://DanSentMe.com/sites/para/resources/allproducts.cfm

The back-cover paint-by-numbers outline will help you focus on what to say to your potential reader and what your book will cover.

Your back cover will contain your most important selling copy. To make the ad-copy writing easier, go to Amazon.com and look for three to five books as close as possible to what you have in mind. Think: if someone bought this book, would they also be interested in mine? Print out the long pages for

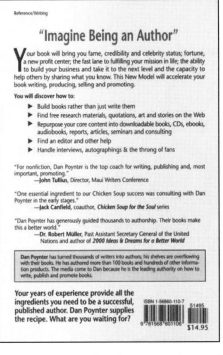

each and use a highlighter to mark the buzzwords and most powerful benefits.

Now turn to your computer, reproduce Document 116 on the screen and fill in the back cover. You will be aided by all the great words written to describe the other books.

You will probably find the draft of your back cover is too long. Now cut out the redundancies and cut the weak parts. It may still be too long and that is OK for now.

Eventually, you will have to draft your back cover anyway. Drafting it before you write your book will help you focus on your readers and will be a guide for you through your book's copy. That will ensure there is a market for your book when you've finish the writing.

As you write your book, you will tweak your back cover and the sales copy will become better and better.

Working title. Drafting your back-cover sales copy will produce several ideas for the title and subtitle. Select a "working title"; something to refer to your book as you write. You may change the title several times before you finish writing the book.

Check Amazon.com to make sure a proposed title has not been used lately. Check 000Domains.com to make sure you can get the URL; register a web domain with the same name. See Document 630 *Selecting a Book Title That Sells* at http://DanSentMe.com/sites/para/resources/allproducts.cfm.

Title Testing. Timothy Ferriss tells of how he used the Internet to decide on a title for *The 4-Hour Workweek*.

He liked one title, his publisher another, and the PR peo ple a third one. Realizing that arguing could be counterproductive, he suggested an objective test. They ran all three in Google ads.

The 4-Hour Workweek (not Tim's favorite) was the winner. Total cost for the test was just over $20.

Try to come up with a title or subtitle that includes a "shelving code" (or BISAC code) and starts with the keyword. See
http://www.bisg.org/publications/bisac_subj_faq.html, and always confirm with a visit to a large bookstore.

Copyright. You may register your copyright before your manuscript is published, but, unless you are passing many copies around for technical proofing and comment, you might just as well do as most publishers do: wait for books to come off the press. Your Work is automatically copyright protected under Common Law the moment you type it because you created it and put it on paper—it just isn't copyright *registered* yet. See
http://www.loc.gov/copyright/, and http://www.loc.gov/copyright/forms/.

The new copyright term is for the author's life plus seventy years. Your ownership of the book is now a valuable part of your estate, so be certain your copyrighted material is mentioned in your will.

To find when copyrighted Works pass into the public domain (how long you will be protected) see
http://www.unc.edu/~unclng/public-d.htm
and
http://www.copyright.cornell.edu/training/Hirtle_Public_D omain.htm.

Using material from others. If you want to use material from another book or website, locate and write to the author; the author (not the publisher) is usually the copyright holder. If the person you want to quote is still living, send him or her the quotation and ask (since some time has passed) if he or she would quote the same thing today? A positive reply provides permission and a paper-trail.

Most authors are thrilled to be quoted as long as you give credit in your text. To locate the author, look for a home town in the About the Author blurb on the back flap or in the front matter of their book. Make an online search. Whitepages.com are helpful

Music is an exception; the owner rarely gives permission to quote lines from a song.

On the other hand, you may just want to use the *ideas* from another book. Copyright covers a sequence of words, it does not cover thoughts. Most books are written from research—from other earlier books. It is permissible to recycle facts and ideas. But do not copy words verba-tim.

When do copyrighted Works pass into the public domain (how long you will be protected)?. See
http://www.unc.edu/~unclng/public-d.htm
and
http://www.copyright.cornell.edu/training/Hirtle_Public_D omain.htm.

If you need a literary attorney to explain this to you, see the lawyers on the Supplier List at
http://parapub.com/sites/para/resources/supplier.cfm.
And, see Document 113 at
http://parapublishing.com/sites/para/resources/allproduct s.cfm.

Using quotations and copyright. Quotations make the text more interesting; your book seems more important; and these words from others confirm your suggestions.

Quotation: Truth well-stated.

Quotations may be sprinkled throughout your text or may be used at the bottom of the pages or on verso (left) pages at the end of chapters—often these are blank pages, so why waste a blank page? Quotations are best used when they are placed nearby to reinforce your words.

Gather quotations as you research your book. It is easy to find what you want online. Search on quotation websites such as http://www.quotegarden.com/

Generally, most quotations are not copyrighted.

a) To copyright words, one must create them *and* put them in "fixed form" such as writing them down or audio-recording them. With quotations, often one person speaks the words and someone else puts them in a book.

b) In most cases, quotations are too short to be subject to copyright.

By the way, the word *quotation* is not the same as the word *quote*, which refers to a price or the cost of a product or service.

Stories. Readers love stories. These accounts help the reader to remember the point you are making; the stories help people associate them with their own lives. Illustrate your helpful informative book with stories from other people's stories and your own. Your stories demonstrate that you are writing from experience; you are an expert on the subject.

Ask colleagues for stories on specific topics. You may also place a (free) request in *Publishing Poynters Marketplace*. See http://parapublishing.com/sites/para/resources/newsletter.cfm.

People want to read something that will help *them*. Unless you are a major celebrity, they do not care about your life story—sorry. So don't call your Work a "memoir." Memoirs are a turnoff to agents, publishers, wholesalers, distributors, bookstores, and buyers. Memoirs are good only for family members.

Write a detailed how-to or self-help book and back up your points with the lessons you've learned through life.

Editing. No writer is so good that he or she should skip editing. We all use editors; well, we all *should* use editors. While the information is yours, rely on a professional wordsmith to check the grammar, syntax, style, and of course punctuation, and spelling. Do not use your old English prof, your secretary, or some "friend" writer you know. Editing is an exacting task that takes years of learning. It is a separate, distinguished profession on its own.

Editors will make copy changes, as well as stylistic, substantive, and structure changes. You should reread the manuscript to make sure the editor has improved the copy without making material changes or introducing new mistakes.

You may save time by submitting your completed manuscript to your copy editor by attaching the manuscript to an email message. If you have a lot of photographs and your manuscript is more than 10 Mb in size, send it on a USB drive or rewritable CD. Have the editor make changes on the file and return it to you. Then re-read the manuscript to make sure the editor improved the copy without making material changes.

If the corrections are made to a printout, you will have to enter the changes and then proof the changes. There are too many new opportunities for new errors.

If you use the Track Changes feature in MS-*Word*, you will have to evaluate all the corrections and re-proof the entire book. You may also find it difficult to delete the embedded changes. Trust your editor. See
See
http://office.microsoft.com/en-us/word/HA010983881033.aspx?pid=CL100636481033

For a list of *book* editors, see
http://parapublishing.com/sites/para/resources/supplier.cfm

Getting feedback on your manuscript
Peer review. One secret to good material is peer review. Smart nonfiction authors take each chapter of their nearly complete manuscript and send it off to at least four experts on that chapter's subject. For more details, see *Writing Nonfiction: Turning Thoughts into Books* by Dan Poynter.

Assessment. Additionally, if you want an assessment on the entire book, contact Gordon Burgett. He will read your book and provide reports on readability and salability. http://www.gordonburgett.com/pathfinder.htm, gordon@gordonburgett.com.

PDF conversion
Using the described system, your manuscript grows looking like a typeset book from the start. Then, with a click of the mouse, you will convert the word-processing file to Adobe Acrobat PDF and you are ready to send the file to a digital book printer for a small quantity of perfect-bound (softcover) books.

If you "pour" your MS *Word* file into a page-layout program, such as InDesign or Quark, the pages will look even better.

For information on PDF, see
http://www.adobe.com/products/acrobat/main.html.

More help with your project

Book Shepherds are a particular kind of consultant. They specialize in taking a book project through all the necessary steps that may include structuring, editing, design, typesetting, locating the right printer, getting a distributor, marketing, and promotion (including your Web presence). Shepherds work with the author/publisher to assure that the book is produced and marketed efficiently and economically. These godparents use their experience and contacts to make sure all the publishing bases are covered and that they are covered in the right order. Some of the better-known Book Shepherds are:

Alan Gadney OneBookPro@aol.com
Barbara Florio Graham (Canada) simon@storm.ca
Barbara Kimmel barbara@nextdecade.com
Bob Goodman rg@silvercat.com
Bobbie Christmas bobbie@zebraeditor.com
Brian Jud iMarketBooks@aol.com
Cynthia Frank Cynthia@CypressHouse.com
Ellen Reid BookShep@mac.com
Ernie Weckbaugh CasaG@wgn.net
Gail Kearns/Penny Paine Gmkea@aol.com
Jacqueline Simonds jcsimonds@beaglebay.com
Jan King jan@eWomenPublishingNetwork.com
Janice Phelps jmp@janicephelps.com
Jim Donovan jdonovan@ptd.net
John Eggen John@MissionMarketingMentors.com
Judith Briles, PhD. judith@briles.com
Kira Henschel Kira@GoblinFernPress.com
Linda Radke info@FiveStarSupport.com
Lisa Pelto Lisa@ConciergeMarketing.com
Maria Carlton (New Zealand), maria@mariacarlton.com
Mary Embree maryembree@sbcglobal.net
Mike Vezo mvezo@mac.com
Mindy Gibbins-Klein (UK) info@bookmidwife.com
Patrick Ang (Singapore) PatAngLH@singnet.com.sg
Rita Mills rmills@ghg.net

Serena Williamson Andrew, PhD. (Canada)
sw@serenawilliamson.com
Sharon Goldinger, pplspeak@norcov.com
Shel Horowitz shel@frugalfun.com
Shum F.P. (Malaysia) shumfp@pd.jaring.my
Simon Warwick-Smith sws@vom.com
Sylvia Hemmerly PubProf@TampaBay.rr.com

The book shepherd is a virtual production and marketing director who is your mentor, tutor, coach, and friend in the book business. Contact them to see what each one can do for you.

If you want help with your editing, proofreading, printing, etc., see our Suppliers List at
http://parapublishing.com/sites/para/resources/supplier.cfm

Consulting
Dan Poynter is available for one-on-one private consulting. He can help you in Santa Barbara, at your place or over the telephone. Most consulting is by telephone. See
http://parapublishing.com/sites/para/speaking/edutrain.cfm

Information kits on specific aspects of books
Each free kit consists of more than fifteen pages of details, tips and resources. Each is geared to a level of The New Book Model/Simultaneous Publishing.

=> Researching and Writing
=> Producing books: printed, LARGE PRINT, eBooks and audiobooks
=> Marketing, promoting & distributing books.
See
http://parapub.com/sites/para/resources/infokit.cfm

Your Writing Assignment

- Research subject.
- Narrow the focus.
- Lay out your binder.
- Draft back-cover sales copy.
- Select a working title.
- Gather quotations.
- Add stories.
- Attack one chapter at a time.
- Don't start writing with chapter one.
- Have the manuscript edited.

Chapter Three

Stage Two
Producing Your Book: Printing, LARGE PRINT, Children's (Color) Books, eBooks, and Audiobooks.

The next step is manufacturing. In this chapter we will discuss printing the book and then we will wring more value out of your Work with more editions.

> The bad news is there are many bad choices.
> The good news is there are many choices.

To make a book go, it has to be read. To break out from the pack of four hundred thousand annually published titles, a book has to reach the Tipping Point or critical mass; it has to benefit from word-of-mouth. To reach bestsellerdom, a book has to be recommended by many people to many other people.

Originally and traditionally, books were printed in hardcover first; the early adopters bought them. A year or so later the book was reissued in softcover. Most people bought the softcover because by then, they'd heard of the book. The budget-minded people waited another couple of years for the mass-market paperback. Those are the smaller-format books printed on pulp paper and sold in drugstores and supermarkets. The conventional wisdom is that one edition does not rob sales from another because the market segments (buyers) are different.

Today, there are more books, published in more editions and available to an even wider audience. For people who spend most of their time at home, the printed-paper book (pBook) is a convenient way to be entertained (fiction) or to learn something/solve a problem (nonfiction). For those in their vehicles such as commuters, sales reps, and long-haul truckers, the audiobook (aBook) works well. For travelers with little room in a suitcase, electronic books (eBooks) fill the bill. For the vision impaired and the reading-challenged, the LARGE PRINT (lpBook) may be the answer.

For example, go to Amazon and look up Dreamcatcher by Stephen King. http://www.amazon.com/Dreamcatcher-Stephen-King/dp/074343627X/.

You will find it available in hardcover, softcover, school/library binding, hardcover/LARGE PRINT, audio cassette, audio CD, audio download and eBook/digital download (.LIT), for the MS-Reader. Stephen King wrote the book once; it is being sold in nine different editions.

If your book is available in more than one edition, it will be read by more people and you are likely to reach the Tipping Point sooner. It does not matter which edition a person reads. He could read the hardcover edition and recommend the title to a colleague who commutes long distances. She could listen to the audio and recommend it to her mother who is sight and hearing impaired. The mother could buy the LARGE PRINT edition and recommend the title to a neighbor who spends a lot of time on airplanes and in airports. He will buy the eBook, and so on. In each case the book is getting read and recommended.

We are distributing entertainment (fiction) or information (nonfiction). We call them "books," but that term is generic; "books" can take many forms. Do not think of your product as a print product—think of it as entertainment or information. Then focus on providing the formats (editions) the buyer wants and needs.

Book production and book selling are changing. Some changes are a benefit and some are a challenge. Publishers cannot alter what is happening in book publishing, but they can use the changes to their advantage.

Typesetting and layout. Your book is now "trial" typeset because you wrote the book by the page rather than by the word. You know how many pages the finished book will be and all the illustrations are in place.

PDF. Almost all files going to book printers today and many eBooks are in Adobe Acrobat Portable Document Format (PDF) form.

You can buy Acrobat, use a service, or, if you are using a typesetter, he or she will take care of creating a PDF formatted file for you.

Adobe Digital Editions. Adobe Digital Editions is a freeware program from Adobe Systems built using Adobe Flash. It is used for acquiring, managing, and reading eBooks, digital newspapers, and other digital publications. The software implements Digital Rights Management and supports PDF, XHTML, and Flash-based content. http://www.adobe.com/products/digitaleditions/ and http://en.wikipedia.org/wiki/Adobe_Digital_Editions.

Book cover. You will need cover art for the book and for online promotion. If you are an artist, you might be able to craft a good cover yourself. See Clipart.com for artwork (illustrations). Some of the subsidy publishers such as Lulu and Wordclay have stock art and cover layout templates.

For a great cover, deal with a book cover artist. They are skilled professionals and know where each element of a cover should be placed. They do not have to be reminded that the cover art may be reproduced in a tiny image online. Go to http://parapublishing.com/sites/para/resources/supplier.cfm. Visit their websites. Select an artistic style that you like.

For more information on covers, see Document 631. See and scroll down at http://DanSentMe.com/sites/para/resources/allproducts.cfm

Money invested in your cover will pay off in sales. Do not skimp on your cover.

Book printing choices. You may turn your book file over to a publisher engaged in author-originated publishing, a subsidy publishing service, a POD printer (using digital presses), a digital book printer or a traditional offset (ink) printer.

Print on demand (POD). But first, a clarification. Print-on-Demand is a way of doing business and *not* a method of printing. POD means receiving an order (with pay-ment), manufacturing the book and then delivering the book.

 Hundreds of years ago, those monks in the abbeys and scribes in the castles were POD publishers. They received an order, manu-factured one book completely by hand and delivered it as requested. The only differ-ence from today's POD publishers was that the monks hand-lettered the pages while today most POD books are manufactured on laser printers in a few minutes.

Print quantity needed (PQN). Traditionally, books were printed in large quantities and sold through bookstores "on spec." In other words, old-fashioned publishers tried to *push* books into the market, rather than let public demand *pull* them through the stores. Those books that did not sell were returned to the publisher and pulped. Some of the larger New York publishers still get 25 percent to 35 percent of their books back. This wasteful practice is very expensive and has to be figured into the cost of the books. It is much more practical to print only the books needed even though the per-unit cost of printing in smaller quantities is higher. Publishers should wait until book sales earn the privilege of a larger print run though proven public demand. This is called *PQN* or Print Quantity Needed.

Use Virtual Book Publishing (VBP) to test the market. When demand increases, switch from POD printing (printing one-at-a-time) to PQN printing. PQN, by the way, may be digital or offset.

> eBooks and POD are tools. Make sure you know how to use them.
> —Mike Shatzkin, PMA Publishing University, 2008

Print run. How many books should you have printed? POD sounds good until you project how many books you will need for initial promotion and consider the cost per unit. Depending upon the number of periodicals serving your potential customers, you may need 300 to 800 books for review copies. Therefore, production through a POD publisher or POD printer may be too expensive. See a digital printer.

Today and in the future, the best system is to print a modest initial print run—say 500 copies to take care of the early demand, and promotion books—such as review copies—and then to print off any further copies from the electronic file on a print-on-demand (POD) basis. The initial print run is used to prime the pump. The money is made in selling the individual copies.

On the other hand, if sales pick up, the publisher can switch over to quantity printing using digital or offset methods.

> There is no "cookie-cutter" solution to the challenge of book production. One size does not fit all. There are many considerations including the needs of your reading audience. Each book is unique and the situation of each author is unique.

Putting a lot of ink on paper is now just an option; a good one if there is large prepublication demand such as advanced sales to bookstores and/or a sale to a book club. Today, with digital (toner) printing, there is no longer a requirement to print 3,000 or more copies of your book "on spec." Here are your choices.

> Offers and business models from publishing-support companies are changing and evolving. Rather than reprinting their current offers, we are listing their URLs so that you can get the latest details directly from them.

A. Subsidy POD Publishers

"POD Publishing" is traditional subsidy or vanity publishing adapting the new technologies of computer typesetting and digital printing. Authors pay for the production and distribution, if any, of their book.

> Can we stop calling subsidies "POD companies"?
> Any publisher, even a traditional publisher, can use POD technology. It is the subsidy arrangement that is the kiss of death, and not the use of digital printing.
> — John Culleton, http://wexfordpress.com

The cost per POD copy may be $5-10 depending upon the number of pages and the trim size of the book. That is much more expensive when compared with the per-unit cost of a similar book printed in greater numbers on an offset press. Printing is a quantity game: the more you print, the less the per-unit cost.

Most vanity/subsidy publishers supply some extra services for their relatively low price. They may take care of the cover, editing, ISBN, Library of Congress number, etc. However, the cover may be pedestrian (being done with stock images in a few minutes), the editing may be minimal (spelling and punctuation at maximum), and the customer service may be close to nonexistent. You aren't paying much and get what you (don't) pay for.

If you deal with a subsidy publisher, you are an "author" and they are the "publisher." Normally, they supply the International Standard Book Number and the ISBN identifies the publisher, not the author. Furthermore, if you win a Ben Franklin Award from the IBPA-Publishers Marketing Association, the award goes to the publisher, not the author or book designer or editor. Thus, this publisher distinction can make a difference.

> Two things about subsidy (AKA POD) publishers.
> They make the easy part, publishing, easier.
> They make the hard part, selling books, harder.
> — John R. Culleton, http://wexfordpress.com

Most subsidy publishers sell more books to their authors than to the public. If you take the number of books they publish and divide by the number of titles, you will find that usually less than 100 books for each title are sold. Their business model is typically structured to produce a profit even when not a single book is sold. Rarely does a subsidized book generate enough in sales to cover the cost of the fees the author has paid to the subsidy publishing service.

Some vanity/subsidy publishers have tarnished records with a lot of unhappy customers. Many customers have complained to the Better Business Bureau and some publishers have been sued. Before dealing with a vanity/subsidy publishing service, make a Google search to check out the company. For example, search for

(That company name) + Scam
(That company name) + Fraud
(That company name) + Rip-off
(That company name) + "Better Business Bureau"

Read the results and be advised.

For a discussion of vanity publishers, see
http://www.aeonix.com/vanity.htm

For an article on how to spot scam vanity/subsidy publishers, see
http://www.wisbar.org/AM/Template.cfm?Section=Wisconsin_Lawyer&template=/CM/ContentDisplay.cfm&contentid=68934

> **Subsidy publishers** are almost always a quick way to disappointment, high costs, and minimal sales.
> — Pete Masterson, *Book Design & Production*.

Since production, printing, and binding cost more than working with a digital printer, the price of the book must either be so high no one will buy it or the author cannot afford to give a discount to stores and other dealers. In fact, most authors are reluctant to purchase copies to send out for review.

Self-publishing is not vanity or subsidy publishing.
Writers are confused and it's not their fault. In searching for the best way to break into print as a published author, they come across self-described "self-publishing companies." I get emails asking if I can self-publish *for* writers. That is physically impossible!

The only "self-publishing company" is you—by definition. If you contract with a publisher, your book is not SELF-published.

The problem is that many vanity/subsidy publishers are calling themselves "self-publishing companies" to make their companies appear more legitimate to aspiring authors eager to be published.

> Self-publishers have been building name recognition for self-publishing for more than thirty-five years. There are more than 85,000 of us in the U.S. Self-publishers, write, publish, and promote their own books.

Now that people know what self-publishing is, we find we have to re-educate the public to the fact that we are the real self-publishers and the other DotCom, digital, subsidy publishers are really just vanity publishers masquerading as us. They are trading on the good reputation we have built.

On the other hand, there are digital printing companies. Most provide excellent prices, service, and quality. They should really refer to themselves as "book printers."

Deal with a subsidy publisher only when you need just a few copies of a book. For example, if you have written a family history, have a very limited budget, and need up to thirty copies for your relatives, the deal offered by most subsidy publishers is hard to beat. But remember, you only get what you pay for; additional services are of questionable value.

Minimum-service versus full-service subsidy publishing

Minimum. With minimum-service firms, there are few if any extra charges. Just upload your text and cover files. If your PDF book file is ready to print, you may deal with a minimum service firm such as Lulu or Createspace. Do-it-yourself/self-service will cost less.

Full. If you need typesetting, editing, cover design, ISBN, etc., you may deal with a company such as Booksurge. The additional services will add to the cost.

A variation is a "book producer" or "book packager" that supplies prepress services. In addition to book design, layout, and typesetting, they can supply printing, design of marketing materials, distribution, fulfillment, setup at Amazon and so on.

For a comparison of the vanity/subsidy publishers' services and pricing as of March 2008, see http://www.selfpublishingnews.wordpress.com/2008/03/05/self-publishing-companies-cost-comparison.html You will also find some companies not listed below.

POD publishers are relatively new so their businesses are evolving. See their websites for information on how they conduct business. For example, some require an exclusive right to use your material and some will not put your ISBN on the back cover.

Here is a list of subsidy publishers. We are mentioning scant information on them because, in many cases, their business plans/way of doing business and offers/prices are evolving. For example, more and more are now offering color printing and some form of distribution. Go to their websites and compare. We do not want you to make a decision based on descriptions that have recently changed.

Check each website. Compare services and costs for printing, types of distribution, promotion, etc. Yes, this will take some time, but you need to learn and compare in order to make an educated decision each individual project.

1. Minimum-Service Subsidy Publishers

With minimum-service firms, there are few if any extra charges.. Just upload your text and cover files.

Booklocker. Angela Hoy is one of the pioneers of publishing using POD technology. She also publishes eBooks. Booklocker has an excellent reputation.
http://www.Booklocker.com

Createspace/Amazon. Like BookSurge, CreateSpace is a subsidiary of Amazon. The difference is that CreateSpace offers fewer services; a good choice if you would rather do many of the prepress jobs yourself. No setup fees.

Access to Amazon distribution is a given. In addition to standard black/white printing, Createspace can produce full-color books; especially important if you publish children's or coffee table books.

http://www.Createspace.com
http://www.createspace.com/Products/BooksOnDemand.jsp;jsessionid=B2E10709EC4C9A370BF01E6E262F39ED.cspworker00

Lulu. There are no setup fees and Lulu is well-known in the business.
http://www.lulu.com

WEbook
http://www.webook.com

Blurb
http://www.blurb.com

2. Full-service subsidy publishers

AuthorHouse/Author Solutions
http://www.authorhouse.com/
http://www.authorsolutions.com/

BookSurge/Amazon. Booksurge is a subsidiary of Amazon; access to Amazon distribution is a given. BookSurge also works with Baker & Taylor; your book is available through B&T on a non-returnable basis.

http://www.BookSurge.com
http://www.booksurge.com/category/2068754161/1/Get-Started.htm

DogEar
http://www.dogearpublishing.net/

Infinity Publishing. Infinity's Author-Originated Publishing program concentrates on selling books to the public as opposed to selling more books and services to the author.

Authors have complete creative control and retain all rights when they grant permission via a non-exclusive agreement to publish and distribute their books in exchange for monthly royalties. Infinity provides distribution through Ingram and participates in Amazon's Advantage program.
http://www.InfinityPublishing.com

iUniverse
in 2008, iUniverse merged with AuthorHouse.
http://www.iUniverse.com

Llumina Press
http://www.llumina.com/index.html

Mill City Press
http://www.millcitypress.net/

Outskirts Press
http://www.outskirtspress.com/

Qoop
http://www.qoop.com/publishing/

Tate Publishing. Specializes in Christian books.
http://www.tatepublishing.com/index.php

Trafford. Provides Ingram distribution and takes part in the Amazon Advantage program.
http://www.Trafford.com

Unlimited Publishing. Unlimited uses Lulu's frêe services exclusively for six to nine months. Books that prove their public appeal by selling just a few hundred copies get an ISBN at LSI-Ingram and replica books-B&T. The others stay at Lulu, where the author, friends, and family can get small quantities as needed, at a decent price with a modest royalty.
http://www.UnlimitedPublishing.com

Virtual Bookworm
http://www.virtualbookworm.com/

Wordclay
http://www.wordclay.com/

Xlibris is part of Authorhouse.
http://www.xlibris.com
http://www2.xlibris.com/

Xulon Press
http://www.xulonpress.com/
Specializes in Christian books.
Xulon prints with LightningSource and distributes through Ingram.

B. Print-on-Demand (POD) Printers

POD printers, like all printers, are in the book manufacturing business and do not invest in the product. They are not "publishers."

The cost per copy may be $5 to $10 depending upon the number of pages and the trim size.

A POD printer is a good option when a book has run its course, your inventory is exhausted and you still receive orders for a couple of copies a month. Rather than invest in inventory, you can have books made one-at-a-time as needed. Don't be left with excess inventory; don't eat the last print run.

POD printers do not own an exclusive on your book or supply the ISBN, They just supply a printing service.

When to use POD printing

a. For bound galleys. When you need a dozen copies for pre-pub reviewers. See Document 112 (frèe) at http://DanSentMe.com/sites/para/resources/allproducts.cfm.

b. For the LARGE PRINT edition.

Some of our books are produced by LightningSource, a POD printer. See *Writing Nonfiction* in LARGE PRINT at http://www.amazon.com/Writing-Nonfiction-Turning-Thoughts-Print/dp/1568601166/.

The LARGE PRINT edition of the book is being *produced* one-at-a-time on demand for Amazon orders. But the book is being *promoted* by sending the regular-print edition to writing, publishing, etc. magazines. There is no need to send reviewers the LARGE PRINT edition.

c. If you run out of offset printed books and do not want to invest in another large print run.

POD printers offer an economical service when you want a single copy of the book at a time.

Here is a list of POD printers:

LightningSource (LSI)/Ingram Book Group offers both production and wholesale availability. With Ingram distribution, your book immediately gets listed and made available to retailers. It *can* be ordered (which is different from it *will* be ordered) from most physical book retailers who have arrangements with Ingram, which is nearly all of them.

LightningSource has plants in the U.S. and U.K. and may open plants in Singapore and Australia. Check their website for news.
http://www.printmediamag.co.uk/market-sector-interviews/245.aspx

http://www.lightningprint.com

Replica Books/Baker & Taylor. Replica is similar to LSI but it makes your book available through Baker & Taylor, the wholesaler. Baker & Taylor will order from LSI if Replica is not producing the book.
http://www.baker-taylor.com
http://www.BTOL.com
http://www.replicabooks.com/

Blitzprint
http://www.blitzprint.com/

C. Digital Printers—Print Quantity Needed (PQN)
Digital printing of multiple copies.

Simultaneous publishing is the New Book Model. For most books, the best system is to print around 500 copies depending upon the number of pre-orders and the quantity of promotional outlets such as category magazines. See
http://parapublishing.com/sites/para/resources/maillist.cfm

After two to three months, you will go back to press for more. At that point, you will be able to make an educated decision on the print run based on the sales rate of the book. Therefore, PQN digital printing is the best way to start. See

The digital process is cost effective for quantities from one hundred to 2,500 copies. If you need more than 2,500, compare costs with offset (ink) printing.

The quality of the toner-based printing is actually better than traditional offset. There are no light and dark pages. The softcover or hardcover books look just like traditional books. Excellent, crisp color covers are usually done with a similar color toner process.

Hardcover. Most books are manufactured with soft covers, called "perfect binding." Hard or "case" binding runs about $1.00 extra per book. That includes the hard covers and the dust jackets. Case binding requires a lot of setup time. Therefore, it rarely pays to put hard covers on a print run of less than three thousand books.

Time Delivery for PQN digitally printed books is normally five days from press proofs; reprints take three to four days. With your disk on file, reprints can be initiated with an email message and the books may be shipped directly to your buyer.

The press proof is usually a single softcover book printed on the same paper stock you propose for the finished book.

The signatures of a digitally printed book are often two pages because most print engines work with cut sheets instead of thirty-two or forty-eight page signatures. Now you do not have to design your book's page count in large signature increments.

Mass customization Since the print engines are computer-driven and because your books can be printed two pages at a time, you may customize the book for your customer. If you make a premium sale to a company, it will cost just pennies to bind in a letter from the CEO or to add the company logo to the cover. You can send the insert or logo to your printer as an email attachment to save time and money.

Cost. What does it cost to manufacture a book? That is like asking, How much is a car? (smile) Each book is unique. Prices will vary with the current cost of paper and labor so use these quoted numbers for comparison only.

For digital printing, the cost may be $3.50 per copy for five hundred books. (Softcover—perfect bound—144-page 5.375" x 8.375" book with black text and a four-color cover.) The per-unit price is higher than for offset printing but you are investing in a smaller number of books and the invoice will be lower.

Digital printers offer an economical service when you want a small inventory of books.

Here is a list of digital printers:

Tri-State Litho
Kumar Persad
71-81 TenBroeck Avenue
Kingston, NY 12401
Tel: 914-331-7581
kumarp@tristatelitho.com
http://www.TriStateLitho.com

BookJustBooks.com
Ron Pramschufer
51 East 42nd Street
New York, NY 10017
Tel: 800-621-2556
customerservice@rjc-llc.com
http://BooksJustBooks.com

Starnet Media Group
P. Jeff DiPaola
50 Commerce Drive
Allendale, NJ 07401-0138
Tel: 201-760-2600
jeff@starnet-media.com
http://www.starnet-media.com

TPC Graphics
Len Metz
518 Coles Mill Road
Haddonfield, NJ 08033
Tel: 856-429-2858
Fax: 856-429-0644
TPClen-Pat@erols.com
Small run digital and conventional book manufacturing. Case, soft binding.

Alexander's Print Advantage
Doyle Mortimer, Barry Merrell
245 South 1060 West
Lindon, UT 84042
Tel: 801-224-8666
Fax: 801-224-0446
eprint@alexanders.com
http://www.Alexanders.com

P.O.D. Wholesale
Mark Gregory – VP Operations
1094 New DeHaven St., Suite 100
West Conshohocken, PA 19428-2713
877-BUY-BOOK
610-941-9999
610-941-9956 FAX
info@podwholesale.com
http://www.podwholesale.com

Morgan Printing and Publishing
Terry Sherrell
900 Old Koenig Lane #135
Austin, TX 78756
Tel: 512-459-5194
Fax: 512-451-0755
terry@morganprinting.org
http://www.MorganPrinting.org

C&M Press
Beth Chapmon
4825 Nome Street
Denver, CO 80239
Tel: 303-375-9922
Fax: 303-375-8699
info@cmpress.com
http://www.cmpress.com/

Sir Speedy-Whittier
Tim McCarthy
7240 Greenleaf Avenue

Whittier, CA 90602
Tel: 562-698-7513
tim@ssWhittier.com
http://www.ssWhittier.com

Sir Speedy-Scottsdale
Mike Bercaw
15776 N 76th Street
Scottsdale, AZ   85260
Tel: 480-947-7277, Ex 111
Fax: 480-946-3957
mBercaw@SirSpeedyScottsdale.com
http://www.SirSpeedy.com/scottsdale

Adibooks
Thomas G. Campbell
181 Industrial Avenue
Lowell, MA 01852
Tel: 978-458-2345
tcampbell@KingPrinting.com
http://www.adibooks.com

BookMobile.com
Nicole Baxter
2402 University Avenue
Saint Paul, MN 55114
Tel: 651-642-9241
Fax: 651-642-9153
nbaxter@bookmobile.com
http://www.BookMobile.com

Documation LLC
Laurene Burchell
1556 International Drive
Eau Claire, WI 54701
Tel: 715-839-8899
Fax: 715-836-7411
lburchell@documation.com
http://www.documation.com

Books-On-Demand
Dave Shannon, CSS Publishing
517 So. Main Street
Lima, OH 45804
Tel: 419-227-1818
http://www.CSSpub.com

aa Printing
William Ashby
6103 Johns Road, #4-5-6
Tampa, FL 33634

Tel: 813-886-0065
Fax: 813-884-0304
bAshby@PrintShopCentral.com
http://www.PrintShopCentral.com

Gorham Printing
Kathleen Shaputis
3718 Mahoney Drive
Centralia, WA 98531
Tel: 1-800-837-0970
Fax: 1-360-273-8679
kathleens@gorhamprinting.com
http://www.gorhamprinting.com

BookMasters, Inc.
2541 Ashland Road
Mansfield, OH 44905
Tel: 800-537-6727
Fax: 419-589-4040
http://www.BookMasters.com

LightningSource/Ingram Book Group
1136 Heil Quaker Boulevard
La Vergne, TN 37086
Tel: 615-213-5815
inquiry@lightningprint.com
http://www.lightningprint.com
Can also make your book available from Ingram (wholesaler).

Printorium Bookworks
A Division of Island Blue Print Ltd.
Bill Green
905 Fort Street,
Victoria, B.C. V8V 3K3
Canada
Tel: 250-385-9786
Tel: 800-661-3332
Fax: 250-385-1377
info@printoriumbookworks.com
www.printoriumbookworks.com

Booksurge/Amazon
Lisa Ryan
5341 Dorchester Road, #16on, SC 29418
Tel: 843-579-0000, Ext 134
Lisa.Ryan@Booksurge.com
http://www.Booksurge.com

AMES On-Demand
Stephen DeForge
12 Tyler Street

Somerville, MA 02143-0120
Tel: 617-684-3611
SDeForge@AMESonDemand.com
http://www.AMESonDemand.com

NetPub
John Dickson
675 Dutchess Turnpike
Poughkeepsie, NY 12603
800-724-1100, ext 347
908-928-0523
jDickson@NetPub.net

U Build a Book
Brian Levine
5217 Verdugo Way, #F
Camarillo, CA 93012
1-866-909-3003
http://www.uBuildAbook.com

Digital Impressions
Karl Buckwalter
1127 International Pkwy, #109
Fredericksburg, VA 22406
Office 540-752-1011
Cell 703-618-4744

360 Digital Books
Keith Reisinger
8089 Stadium Drive, Suite C
Kalamazoo, MI 49009
Tel: 866-379-8767
Fax: 734-591-7899
kreisinger@360inc.com
www.360digitalbooks.com

Imaging Hawaii
Terry Lau
P. O. Box 22790
Honolulu, HI 96823
terry@imaginghawaii.com
http://www.imaginghawaii.com/

D. Offset Printers and Ink Printing with Plates

Deal with an offset printer when you need 2,500 books or more. Some offset printers will print as few as five hundred copies but they are most efficient when printing thousands.

Costs. For offset printing, the cost may be $1.25 per copy for three thousand books. Softcover—"perfect bound"—144 page 5.375" x 8.375" book with black text and a four-color cover. Offset printers offer an economical service when you need a larger inventory of books.

See the list of offset printers in *The Self-Publishing Manual*, Document 603: *Book Printing at the Best Price* or the *Buying Book Printing* report at http://DanSentMe.com/sites/para/resources/allproducts.cfm

Beware of cross-grain printing More and more printers are cheating; they are manufacturing books incorrectly.

Paper has a grain—just like wood. The paper in a book should have its grain oriented vertically or top to bottom. If the paper's grain is positioned horizontally, the book will have a strange feel to it. The book will not "roll" open and will want to snap shut. Your customers and bookstore browsers will not know what the "problem" is but they will subconsciously feel that something is odd about your book. It will make them uncomfortable. And—you may lose the sale.

When you send the request for quotations (RFQs) to printers, specify "right grain" printing. Printers know the difference. Let them know that you know the difference. Get all you are paying for.

Producing LARGE PRINT Books (lpBooks)

You can make your book available for the visually impaired and the reading challenged by simply changing the parameters in Adobe Acrobat when you convert the file to PDF. Then the book is printed in larger format (8.5 x 11). While all the pages in both the regular and LARGE PRINT editions are the same. There is no need to re-typeset, re-index or change the table of contents.

Convert the page-layout file to PDF. Load Adobe Acrobat. Click on File\Print to bring up the Print Dialog box. Set the printer name to Adobe PDF. Check the *Fit to Paper* option. Recheck the typesetting; the type usually moves. *Fit to Paper* will enlarge the smaller (5.5 x 8.5) format to fit the 8.5 x 11 paper.

You may use a digital printer for your regular-size book and a POD printer such as LightningSource for the LARGE PRINT edition.

For details on producing large PRINT (lpBooks), see Document 642 Large PRINT Books at
http://parapub.com/sites/para/resources/allproducts.cfm

As mentioned above, some of our books are produced by LightningSource, a POD printer. See *Writing Nonfiction* for an example of large PRINT at
http://www.amazon.com/Writing-Nonfiction-Turning-Thoughts-Print/dp/1568601166/

Producing Children's Books

Illustrated children's books belong in a special category due to their format, color pictures and audience. Printing color costs more; printing color with offset (ink) printing is very expensive. Printing color books digitally is not too expensive for promotional copies but is not economical for for-sale copies. Children's books do not command a high price.

Thousands of people have written children's picture books that will never be published. Nothing is wrong with the books—many are very good; the barriers are too high. The publishers are swamped with submissions and the $20,000+ production cost is a huge investment.

People buy $3.1 billion of children's books annually; the market is huge. The books sell for an average $7.34 in softcover and $14.51 in hardcover. It is hard to make money when 4-color printing is so expensive and a minimum pressrun is 3,000 books.

In 2008, the Consumer Product Safety Improvement Act (CPSIA) went into effect requiring that books be certified as lead-free. The law places a huge additional expense on printed children's books. See http://thephoenix.com/Boston/News/74940-Congress-bans-kids-from-libraries/

Rather than investing in printed books, the children's book author is encouraged to lay out the book in Power-Point. This multimedia program allows the addition of video, animations, sound and hot hyperlinks to more information. Your children's book can be interactive; the child can click on icons for more information, a different story line, animations and sound. The book can even be personalized, making the child the main character. Children love computers and they find reading on a screen irresistible.

This is not a new way of printing; it is a whole-new approach that is more versatile, more fun for the child and a whole lot less expensive. The reproduction cost of a CD is about 35 cents per copy.

For color printing, see

Sir Speedy-Whittier
http://www.ssWhittier.com

CreateSpace
http://www.CreateSpace.com

To create your children's book online, see
http://www.biguniverse.com/

For more resources for children's books, see
Document 610. See and scroll down at:
http://parapublishing.com/sites/para/information/writing.cfm

Producing Electronic Books (eBooks)

The traditional method of disseminating written entertainment, called "fiction" and written information, called "nonfiction" is no longer working.

While we will always have print, the future is in the electronic dissemination of "books". Electronic distribution is faster, easier and less expensive. It shortens the time between author and reader.

My own experience indicates that eBook sales do not cannibalize paper book sales.
--Morris Rosenthal, Foner Books.

eBooks are finally turning the corner. The hardware and software have been around for years. Now more and more content is becoming available. eBook sales are increasing for environmental reasons, due the cost of (truck) transportation and the recent closing of many brick & mortar book and other stores.

The reasons eBooks did not take off in the 90's were lack of content, digital rights management (DRM) and High pricing.

Industry eBook sales are growing; up 37 percent in 2007. See http://BookStatistics.com
http://www.openebook.org/doc_library/industrystats.htm
The clout of Sony with their Reader, the content of Amazon with their Kindle, the flexibility of MobiPocket, and the smooth delivery system of FictionWise are getting a lot of press. The public consciousness of eBooks is being raised.

The large-screen Kindle makes the transition from printed books to eBooks easier and the purchasing of books much faster. Why put POD printing machines in every bookstore? When clients have eBook readers, they do not have to visit a bookstore.

College textbooks may go digital very soon and very quickly. That will solve some of the textbook price and distribution challenges as well as providing a cost-effective means to keep the content current. See http://ahcilunch.blogspot.com/2008/03/student-watch-survey-updates-digital-ed.html

eReaders are becoming more sophisticated, the volume of content is increasing, standards are emerging, digital rights management (DRM) is becoming less cumbersome.

eBook Hardware. The most popular eBook readers are:
Amazon Kindle
iPhone
Pocket PC
Readius. Has a roll-out screen. http://www.polymervision.com/
Sony Reader

Sony has developed a flexible, full-color paper screen. See http://www.youtube.com/watch?v=k6bkmPjVF-k

If a major reason for writing your book is to establish credibility in your field, your book must also be in print.

eBook Format. Many eBooks consist of broad pages of boring type. They are not produced in page-layout for-mat. Most people do not want to read large pages with wall-to-wall type. That looks like a manuscript—not a book.

Your pBook and eBook should look the same. If you write your printed book first and do so in page-layout format, you will finish your eBook at the same time. When read in a smaller format such as on an iPhone or Pocket PC, the text is re-flowed to fit the screen on loading.

eBook Software. There are many different eBook reader software formats. Some can be used on more than on type of hardware device.

eReader [-er.PDB] iPhone

Adobe [.PDF]
Microsoft [.LIT]
Palm Doc [.PDB]
Rocket/REB1100 [.REB]
Franklin [.FUB]
Hiebook [.KML]
Sony Reader [.LRF]
Isilo [-IS.PDB]
Mobipocket [.PRC]
Kindle [.MOBI]
OEBFF Full VGA [.IMP]
OEBFF Half VGA [.IMP]

See
http://www.fictionwise.com/help/ebook-formats-faq.htm

EPUB file format. EPUB is a reflowable XML-based file format sponsored by the International Digital Publishing Forum (IDPF) which is catching on with publishers. It is proposed that publishers will convert their print books into EPUB first. Then distributors or retailers could convert the EPUB file to other formats such as Mobipocket or Palm—whatever the customer might want. EPUB can be read but it is designed to be converted to other formats. See
http://www.idpf.org

For more information, request the EPUB whitepaper from EPUB@Overdrive.com

BookDROP. A standard designed to streamline how online book content is shared between publishers with digital book content repositories.

http://www.publishersweekly.com/article/CA6621664.htm
l

Turning pages. With Flip@Once page-turning technology, you can create eBooks from PDF files. Converted
documents can be read online or off and you can see the
pages turn.
http://FlipAtOnce.com

iPhone. One of the reason's for the
iPhone's phenomenal success is the App
Store. In less than five months, more than
10,000 Apps became available. Two of
those Apps are the eReader and Stanza.
Many analysts estimate within next 2 years
the iPhone Apps will be a Billion Dollar Industry.

The multifunction iPhone provides a very
nice reading device. For a video demo of the eReader, see
http://www.fictionwise.com/help/iphoneFaq.htm

iPhone forum.
http://www.talkiphone.com/forums/iphone-chat/244-
ebook-reader.html

See the file conversion resources below. In addition, you will have to submit an icon for your
eBook. See

http://www.softfacade.com/blog/15_free_icon_sets_for_i
phone

http://fortysevenmedia.com/blog/archives/custom_webcli
p_icons_for_your_iphone_or_ipod_touch_home_screen/

For an icon artists, see Robert Howard,
http://www.BookGraphics.com

Cell-phone novels. Four of the five best-selling novels in Japan in 2007 belonged to an entirely new literary form called keitai shosetsu: novels written, and read, on cell phones. 86% of high school, 75% of middle school and 23% of grade school girls read cell phone novels. Ten of Japan's print bestsellers in 2007 were based on cell phone novels--successfully selling about 400,000 copies apiece. One company has released 40 titles that have sold 10 million copies. See
http://www.newyorker.com/online/blogs/books/2008/12/phoning-it-in.html

File conversion services
Some file converters are listed here. Most can convert your MS-*Word* or PDF file to .LIT, .PDF, Kindle, Mobi-Pocket, Palm, Blackberry, etc. editions or formats. Some details are provided here but check their websites as the services are growing, changing and evolving.

Some of these converters can also provide distribution; make your eBook file available to several eBook online stores.

Smashwords is a free platform for publishing eBooks. You upload your Microsoft Word file into their system and they automatically convert that file into about 10 different eBook formats so these books can be read on the iPhone, on the Amazon Kindle and on virtually any other eBook reading device. The DRM-free formats include EPUB used by the Stanza reading software. eBooks are sold online via Stanza and the Smashwords online bookstore. There are no setup or conversion fees; Smashwords takes 15% of the net sales.

With Smashwords, the author owns the copyright, owns all the rights to the work and sets their own price for the book and the sampling privileges.
http://SmashWords.com
http://www.smashwords.com/signup/login/upload

http://www.siliconvalley.com/news/ci_11409483?nclick_check=1
http://blog.smashwords.com/2009/01/rise-of-ebooks-idpf-reports-ebook-sales.html

Publishing Dimensions converts hardcopy and electronic files into all eBook, POD and print formats.
http://www.PubDimensions.com
info@pubdimensions.com

DetailsPlease will convert your book to an eBook for Amazon Kindle, Sony Reader, Mobipocket and Palm OS. They charge a fee for conversion but do not take a percentage of sales.
http://detailsplease.com/Ebook/
Tel: 815-550-2791

codeMantra provides a complete prepress-to-postpress content management solution. They convert to PDF and XML.
http://www.codeMantra.com
US: cminfo@codemantra.com
UK: euroinfo@codemantra.com

eBookApp.com converts doc, txt, rtf, and html files into iPhone format and uploads them to the iPhone/Tunes Store for purchase. The author sets the price and can track sales. eBookApp.com charges a conversion fee and takes a percentage of sales.
http://eBookApp.com

eChapterOne.com converts to PDF, LIT and Palm formats with DRM and posts the files at LightningSource (LSI) and their own bookstore. The author selects the list price.
http://www.echapterone.com/store/authorpublisher.asp

Ingram Digital Digitizes, inventories and distributes eBooks.
http://www.IngramDigital.com

ask@ingramdigital.com

AppEngines converts plain text, Word or RTF to the iPhone/iPod Touch devices and sets up the eBook in the iTunes App Store. No charge for the conversion and distribution. App Engines takes a percentage of the price on a sliding scale depending upon the list price.

http://www.appengines.com/
info@appengines.com
Tom Peck: tPeck@appengines.com

ScrollMotion uses its Iceberg system to convert files for eBooks on the iPhone and iPod Touch. Plans are to expand output to Google's G-1/Android and the Blackberry. Scrollmotion eBooks come with reading software and do nor require a separate software program. Book purchase downloads are made over a Wi-Fi connection.
http://www.scrollmotion.com/
info@scrollmotion.com

Shortcovers, from Canada's Indigo Book & Music chain-store is a website with a companion iPhone app. Short-covers supports the EPUB standard and makes eBooks available with or without DRM.
http://shortcovers.com/splash/
http://blog.shortcovers.com/

Amazon.com
Kindle and MobiPocket only.
http://www.Amazon.com

Electronic & Database Publishing
http://www.ElectronicAndDatabasePub.com

Read How You Want
Can also get Australian books into Amazon.
http://www.ReadHowYouWant.com

Texterity creates, delivers and tracks digital editions of magazines. Periodicals can be viewed on computers, iPhones and iPod touch devices. Offices in the US, Canada and Australia.
http://www.Texterity.com

File conversion programs (DIY)
You may also make eBook file conversions yourself.

DropBook turns Word documents into PDB files.
http://pwp.netcabo.pt/gorod/publishebook/download.htm

Blackman's eBook Converter is a free program.
http://www.softpedia.com/get/Others/E-Book/Blackman-s-eBook-Converter.shtml

Feedbooks (http://feedbooks.com/share/): You can log into Feedbooks and create your own content, which will be made available in EPUB, as well as other formats such as PDF and Kindle. In addition, any books you create and share will automatically be included in the "Free Books by Feedbooks" section of Stanza's Online Catalog under the "User Created Books" area, so you don't need to download and transfer the book separately.

eReader
http://www.ereader.com/ereader/help/dropbook/

Stanza Desktop (http://stanza.lexcycle.com): Stanza, from Lexcycle, allows you to convert from a large variety of formats like MS LIT, Mobipocket, Kindle, RTF, PDF, MS Word, and many more into EPUB. Stanza has partnered with Fictionwise on eBook distribution.

Adobe InDesign
 (http://www.adobe.com/products/indesign/): InDesign is a high-end publishing tool for authors and publishers, and supports the creation of EPUB files.'

Calibre (http://calibre.kovidgoyal.net/): a free tool for Windows, Mac OSX, and Linux that allows you to convert to ePub from a wide variety of formats. Some say that Calibre currently does a better job than Stanza Desktop at preserving styles and formatting of source documents.

BookGlutton API. If your book is in HTML format, you can convert it into EPUB using their online conversion API. http://www.bookglutton.com/api

LightningSource (LSI), a subsidiary of Ingram, is an eBook distributor.

LSI accepts uploads in PDF, LIT (Microsoft) and PDB (Palm) formats. LSI will list your title in its catalog and make it available to large resellers including Amazon.com, Powells Books, Ebookmall, Diesel Ebooks, and others. The agreement with LSI is non-exclusive; you can deal with other distributors.

More information on eBooks
Join the E-book community on Yahoo:
http://groups.yahoo.com/group/ebook-community/

http://www.publishyourownebooks.com/

Producing Audiobooks (aBooks)

Once your book is written, you have a script for the audio edition. Your audio product may be put on a CD, DVD and/or sold as a download. The download avoids packaging and shipping.

Audiobooks can be listened to on many devices including the iPhone and Pocket PC.

Here are some recording choices.

Record the book yourself or hire a student (intern?) "voice talent" from the communications department of a local college.

All you need are a microphone, recording/editing software and a hard disk for storage. If you do not already have a mic, they are about $30 at Radio Shack and other electronic outlets.

A frèe software program is Audacity. See
http://audacity.sourceforge.net/

There are text to speech programs but they do not yet sound normal. Listen to samples on the site.
http://www.nuance.com/realspeak/word/

Once you have your MP3 files completed, you may upload them for sale as a CD or download.

You can record a bare-bones MP3 audio edition without special equipment at AudioAcrobat.com. It is often a good idea to record one chapter at a time.
http://www.AudioAcrobat.com

Spoken Books Publishing, a division of Infinity Publishing. Infinity records, edits, manufactures, distributes and sells.
http://www.spokenbookspublishing.com/
CreateSpace.
http://www.createspace.com/Products/CDOnDemand.jsp; jsessionid=B2E10709EC4C9A370BF01E6E262F39ED.cspworker00

Amazon.com. Amazon bought Audible and sells downloads as well as audiobooks on tape and CD.
http://www.Amazon.com

Lulu
http://www.Lulu.com

Kunaki
http://www.Kunaki.com

PODiobooks. At PODiobooks, you can serialize chapters of your book as a sales tool for the full Work.
http://podiobooks.com

For more information on how to produce audiobooks, see Document 635 *AudioBooks; Turning Books & Speeches Into Spoken-Word Download & Disc Products* at http://DanSentMe.com/sites/para/resources/allproducts.cfm

The International Standard Book Number (ISBN)

The ISBN is a world-wide identification system which has been in use since the late sixties. There is a different ISBN for each edition and each binding of every book so the number's use avoids errors in identifying the books ordered, shipped, received, etc. Publishers are finding this system has become an essential element in the distribution and tracking of their books.

The charge varies depended on how many numbers you want. Contact the ISBN Agency.
http://www.isbn.org/standards/home/index.asp

Once started in the system, you will assign each of your new titles an ISBN suffix yourself. You do not have to start at the beginning of the log; the only requirement is that you assign a different ISBN to each *edition* of each book: softcover, hardcover, audiobook, downloadable, CD, etc. If you use the first number of the block, the "0" at the end of the string will tip off those in the industry that this is a first book.

Bar codes. The bar code on a book identifies the ISBN, which in turn identifies the publisher, title, author and edition (hardcover, etc.). The wholesalers, chains and other bookstores will not accept your book or audiobook without a bar code. If your book arrives at a wholesaler without a bar code, they will sticker it and charge you for the service. Further, since most books have bar codes, it will look odd without one—and it will not be taken seriously.

The barcode you want is the "Bookland EAN/13 with add on" and it should be printed on the lower half of "cover 4" (the back cover) on hardcover and softcover books and on cover 2 (the inside of the front cover) on mass-market paperback books.

On mass-market paperbacks (usually sold in drug and grocery stores), the UPC barcode goes on the back cover. It is quite doubtful you will need a UPC bar code.

The ISBN is printed above the bar code. You can get both the barcode and ISBN typeset at one place. Use the ISBN on invoices, catalogs, order forms, packing lists and the book itself. Use the bar code (with the ISBN) on the back cover of the book.

See http://www.bisg.org/isbn-13/index.html

Note the difference in the last digits

On January 1, 2007, ISBN agencies all over the world assigned new ISBN numbers that are 13 digits long, replacing the 10 digit numbers previously provided. Eventually, new blocks will be prefixed with 979 instead of the current 978. See
http://www.isbn-13.info/index.html
http://www.tux.org/~milgram/bookland/

So, the bar coder reads the 13-digit 978 ISBN as always. But for a while longer, the industry needs the 10-digit ISBN positioned across the top of the bar code too.

Bar code/ISBN prints, self-adhesive labels and negatives cost $10-$30 and are available from the suppliers listed at:
http://parapublishing.com/sites/para/resources/supplier.cfm

Assign an ISBN to your book, order a bar code negative and give it to your cover artist for incorporation into your back cover design.

For barcode software, see http://www.newfreedownloads.com/find/ean-barcode.html

Standard Address Number. The SAN identifies each separate address of every firm in the book publishing industry from publishers, to wholesalers, to libraries, to bookstores. SANs sort out the billing and shipping addresses and help to determine which "Book Nook" an order is going to.

A SAN may be requested when you apply for an ISBN. The seven-digit number should be printed on all stationery, purchase orders, invoices, etc.

Advanced Book Information. By filling out the ABI form, your book will be listed in *Books in Print* and several other specialized directories.
http://www.booksinprint.com/bip/

Bowkerlink publisher access system. BowkerLink is a free online access system that provides you with an automated tool to add titles to *Books In Print*® as well as update any records that are already listed.
http://www.bowkerlink.com/corrections/common/home.asp.

Library of Congress Preassigned Control Numbers. The LCCN or PCN number appears on the copyright page of each book. The PCN differs from the ISBN in that one ISBN is assigned to each different *edition* of a work (hardcover, softcover, etc.); the PCN number is assigned to the Work itself, no matter how the books are printed or bound. PCN numbers are essential if you want to sell to libraries.

The PCN must be requested prior to the publication of the book so that the number may be printed on the copyright page. The Copyright Office does not provide numbers to books that are already in print (it is too late to print the number in the book).

New publishers should contact the Copyright Office, http://www.LOC.gov or http://www.loc.gov/loc/infopub/.

You must complete the Application to Participate and obtain an account number and password. Then you can apply for a PCN. Then the Library of Congress will send you your number. See
http://pcn.loc.gov/pcn/pcn007.html and
http://ecip.loc.gov/pls/ecip/pub_signon?system=pcn

The first two digits of the PCN number do not indicate the year of publication, but the year in which the card number is preassigned. If you register after January 1, your book will appear to be a year newer. Ever wonder why the dates on films are in Roman numerals?

Chapter Four

Stage Three
Distributing Your pBook, eBook, etc.

I f you did the subject research outlined in Chapter Two, you have a good idea of where your markets are and how to reach them.

Dealers
The only way to extend your reach and sell more books is through dealers. Dealers are rewarded for their efforts by earning a discount on quantity purchases of books.

Don't focus on the amount you must give to dealers as a discount. Remember, printing is a quantity game, the more books you print, the lower the per-unit cost. So use dealers, sell more books, reach more readers and pay less per book for their manufacture.

Selling through affiliates
Another way to expand the exposure for your book is to allow others sell your book as dealers. One form of deal-ership is an affiliation.

Affiliations work better with eBooks than pBooks because most affiliates want you to drop ship the printed books. That is, they send you the shipping slips and you have to wrap and ship the book. You wind up doing the shipping of the single book and you make less on the sale.

People may contact you about affiliating and/or you may find affiliates/dealers though an affiliate brokerage company such as ClickBank. See
http://www.ClickBank.com

Distributing Paper books
The Book Trade consists of distributors, wholesalers and bookstores. There are three types of bookstores: Chain such as Barnes & Noble, independent such as the tattered Cover in Denver and online such as Amazon. To reach the Book Trade, we used to recommend using a distributor.

Some of the challenges today are
  Independent store sales in the U.S. are down to 9 percent and they are decreasing.

  Chain store sales in the US are at 33 percent and they are decreasing.

  Online store sales in the U.S. are at 31 percent and they are on the increase.

> Tolerate brick & mortar bookstores, don't pursue them.

More and more book sales are made online as opposed to brick & mortar stores. The handwriting is on the (virtual) wall; this is the future of book/information purchasing.

According to Forrester Research, people shop online for the following reasons:
  49 percent for convenience
  46 percent for the greater selection
  43 percent for lower prices

It makes more sense to sell where the customers are and will be. Pursue online sales, maintain smaller inventories of books and promote the books online. Make books available through bookstores but concentrate on non-Book Trade promotion and sales.

People are creatures of habit; they buy books where they usually buy books. Some frequent a nearby book-shop in their lunch hour, some make purchases online, some deal directly with the publisher and so on. You aren't likely to change these buying patterns. If your books are not available in stores, from you, from Amazon, etc., you will not get every sale from each promotional program you spend time and money on. Your book has to be available everywhere to reach the entire audience.

Before you sign with a POD publisher, check on the distribution they offer. At a minimum, you want paper book availability through wholesalers Ingram and Baker & Taylor and online booksellers Amazon.com and BarnesAndNoble.com.

Without Ingram, your book will not appear on many of the major eRetailer websites, such as Barnes & Noble. This is because of the widespread use of the Ingram book database.

Most digital printers do not offer distribution to the book trade; they are printers only.

Be aware that some booksellers require a US bank account and a US address. If you are outside of the US, check for Nexus, a connection; see if they have a branch in your country. If so, the U.S. company should accept you.

For example, if there is a BookSurge in your country, you can get access to Amazon in the U.S.

To get into Amazon, you can go through BookSurge or CreateSpace. CreateSpace has an international plan that does not require a U.S. address or bank account.

Australians can also get access to Amazon through
http://www.ReadHowYouWant.com

Distributors

Most distributors take 66 percent of the list price of the book. They have reps that visit the stores, show your covers, warehouse and ship your books. For a list of distributors to the Book Trade, see *The Self-Publishing Manual*, Volume 1, *Book Marketing* report or Document 605 at http://DanSentMe.com/sites/para/resources/allproducts.cfm

Wholesalers

There are two major wholesalers in the U.S.—Ingram and Baker & Taylor. Ingram is strongest with stores and B&T has traditionally been number-one with libraries. Wholesalers do not have sales reps. They just ship when an order is received.

Each of these wholesalers has print-on-demand printing subsidiaries. Using their printing facilities, you can avoid carrying inventory and shipping books to them. When they get an order for one of your books, they will manufacture it and deliver it. Then they will remit your cut of the money to you.

Ingram. LightningSource is a POD printer that is a subsidiary of Ingram. It is widely used.

Sign up with LightningSource and serve Ingram through LSI. Go to http://www.LightningSource.com. Read and sign their four contracts for POD printing and eBook distribution in the U.S. and the U.K. Soon, there should be eight contracts when LSI moves into Australia and Singapore. Once LSI sends your ID and password, you can upload your text and cover files to their website.

Baker & Taylor. Replica Books is a POD printer that is a subsidiary of Baker & Taylor. They work on an exclusive or nonexclusive basis. Read and sign their contract. Then upload your text and cover files to their website.

Be aware, that Replica wants to deal with publishers that have a number of out-of-print books and may not take you. But, B&T will purchase from LightningSource.

This site is currently under construction at www.replicabooks.com/

Independent Book Stores

Most independent stores are struggling. Approach the following large stores plus those in your hometown. Be aware that they will probably ask, "Where can I get your book?" Not from you but from a wholesaler they deal with regularly such as Ingram. Here are a couple of larger independent stores:

   📖 Powell's in Portland, Oregon
      http://www.powells.com

   📖 Tattered Cover in Denver, Colorado.
      http://www.tatteredcover.com

Chain Book Stores

The larger chain stores—Borders, Barnes & Noble, and Books-a-Million—sell nearly one-quarter of the books in the U.S.

Approach the chain stores directly. Contact their headquarters' book buyers by telephone or with a visit. Do not make an appointment with the Small Press buyer. Contact the buyer for your *category* of book.

Barnes & Noble

B&N is the major chain store in the U.S. and has an online presence (B&N.com).

Barnes & Noble Booksellers
Marcella Smith, Vendor Relations
122 Fifth Avenue
New York, NY 10011
Tel: 212-633-3300; Tel: 212-807-0099; Tel: 212-253-0810 (Corporate Headquarters).
Send your book, marketing plan, and anything else to help Marcella Smith decide to accept the book.

Borders

During the last half of 2008 and into 2009, Borders was struggling to survive and was up for sale. Avoid Borders until their situation shakes out.

Borders Group, Inc.
Kelley Wardzala, or category buyer (Call for the current name), New Vendor Acquisition
100 Phoenix Dr.
Ann Arbor, MI 48108-2202
Tel: 734-913-1100, Fax: 734-477-1100

Books-A-Million

http://www.booksamillion.com

Chapters/Indigo, Inc. is a Canadian chain store expanding into airport shops in the U.S.

Chapters, Inc.
90 Ronson Dr.
Etobicoke, ON M9W 1C1
Canada
Tel: 416-243-3138, Fax: 416-243-8964
http://www.chapters.indigo.ca/?pticket=1gskpnapctpzgp3
4a52f0bvrhi2PEweV5LfZH%2fsc5ckVaWR%2b7Wo%3d

Doubleday Bookshops
122 Fifth Ave.
New York, NY 10011
Tel: 212-633-3300

Another way to get into chain stores is to offer a mini seminar on your subject. We used to call these "auto-graphings."

Then you must turn out the crowd. Remember, the store is only providing the venue. They want you to bring in new customers.

Send an announcement to everyone in your email address book and ask your friends, relatives, and colleagues to forward the announcement to anyone they know (within driving distance) who will be interested in you or the subject. Take books to the store.

When you get to the store, proceed to the shelf where your book will be and look for other books very much like yours.

Take them back to the presentation/autographing area. During your mini seminar, take time to hold up the other books (puts your book in good company) and praise them.

"This is the book that got me started in this business."
"This is the book I keep next to my dictionary for constant reference," and so on.

Your audience can purchase just your book or they can leave the store with three or four. Each person can spend $20 or $60. Sixty dollars will impress the store a lot more. And that store will want to stock your book.

Then go to the next chain store. Based on your prior performance, they will want you; they may even have heard of you already. After a few stores, the chain will want your book.

Do not be disappointed when the chain puts you in three hundred stores instead of every one of their eight hundred outlets. Each store is profiled; they know what will sell in that neighborhood. For example, a business title will go into downtown stores while parenting titles will be displayed in stores in the suburbs. Your books will go into the stores were it will move.

> It's the author, not the book.
> Stores want authors who sell books.
> Books don't sell themselves, authors sell books.

Online Book Stores

As of this writing Amazon.com accounts for nearly 20 percent of the sales of books in the U.S. Barnes&Noble.com has a much smaller share.

Amazon.com
Approach through Booksurge.com or CreateSpace.com. Use CreateSpace if you do not have a U.S. address and a U.S. bank account.

Amazon wants you. They have infinite shelf space. If you do not notify Amazon of your book, they will find you— eventually. Log onto Amazon, scroll to the bottom of the page and click on *Sell Items*.
Also see
http://www.amazon.com/gp/seller-account/mm-summary-page.html

http://www.amazon.com/Money-home-page/b/ref=gw_m_b_si?ie=UTF8&node=3309511

Check Amazon for:

— Amazon Advantage. You ship to Amazon. (They maintain physical inventory— not using on-demand printing as the orders come in).
Amazon processes the orders, picks, packs, ships, and bills.

— Amazon Affiliate. Double dip. Become an Amazon Affiliate and then when a buyer goes from your website to Amazon, you get a 7 percent cut of the sale.

— Amazon Marketplace. With Marketplace, they take the order, send it to you, you pick, pack, and ship. They collect the money and send it to you, less a fee, but adding in a shipping allowance for you. See
http://www.amazonsellercommunity.com/forums/index.jspa

— Fulfillment by Amazon (FBA). They store the product (you ship to them), they receive the order from any channel, pick, pack, and ship. You manage the billing and collections. Amazon is a fulfillment center.
http://www.amazon.com/gp/seller/fba/fba_step3.html

Amazon Author Stores Pages on Amazon are devoted to all of an author's Works. Each Author Store includes a bibliography, and can include a biography, author photo, and discussion board.
http://www.publishersweekly.com/article/CA6625547.html
http://www.amazon.com/gp/feature.html?ie=UTF8&docId=1000286411

Barnes & Noble.com
http://www.BarnesAndNoble.com

Fulfillment houses

Fulfillment houses will pick, pack and ship both individual and bulk orders.

Atlas/BookMasters eliminates seasons, avoids pubdates, has a connection with Ingram and gets your books listed everywhere.
http://www.BookMasters.com.

Book Clearing House has a connection to Ingram.
http://www.BookCH.com

Non-traditional Book Markets

For most well-targeted "Long Tail" books, far more sales will be made to stores, catalogs, etc. outside the traditional Book Trade. For example, Skydiving books can be sold to parachute catalogs, skydiving schools, skydiving clubs, and parachute magazines, etc. These dealers buy in large quantities, feel a 40 percent discount is a good deal, pay in thirty days and never return a book.

Amazon, Google and the many search engines make books on any subject easier to find.

The secret to nontraditional book sales is to identify and locate your market. Be realistic about the (small) group of people who are vitally and personally interested in the subject. Then try to locate them. Ask yourself: what stores do they shop in, what magazines do they read, what associations and clubs do they join and, even, what TV channels (golf or history for example?) do they watch? Approach your prospective buyers where you can find a high concentration of them. Go to places where your potential readers have voluntarily come together to form groups of like-minded people. Dig your mine where the ore is richest.

If you are selling into your own industry, this will be easy. You can look into the mirror and see a reflection of your customer.

See the *Book Marketing* report at http://DanSentMe.com/sites/para/resources/allproducts.cfm

ebook Distribution

Once your book is ready for the printer, you will have the file for the eBook, it is nearly done. See the previous chapter on eBook file conversion. Some of the file converters offer distribution to some dealers. Here are the major distributors of eBooks. Some offer conversion services as well.

http://www.LightningSource.com
http://www.Overdrive.com
http://www.ReadHowYouWant.com (Australia)

Downloading from your own site is not recommended. You want your eBook sold by eStores with high volumes of traffic and you want as many resellers (dealers) as feasible. You want your eBook to be exposed to as many potential customers as possible.

It is not likely that your site has the traffic these dealers have. Additionally, if you offer downloads, you will receive many customer service calls (to your toll-free number) from people who are unable to find the eBook they just downloaded. It is far better to prompt clients to click through from your site to one of the dealers.

ebook websites

Your eBook should be in as many formats as possible and sold through as many eBook store outlets as possible in order to reach a maximum number of buyers.

To see how some of the major online resellers are mer-
chandising eBooks, see the following sites. In many
cases, look for an ebook tab.

Amazon.com. (Kindle and MobiPocket formats).
http://www.Amazon.com

BookLocker (PDF only)
http://www.booklocker.com/getpublished/published.html

Powells.com
http://www.powells.com/ebookstore/ebooks.html

Palm
http://www.ereader.com/welcome

Adobe Digital Media Store
http://www.adobe.com/products/digitaleditions/library/

FictionWise. A major retailer with offerings in several
formats.

Fictionwise Secure **eReader** titles are encrypted eBooks
that can be read with free eReader Pro software. The
eReader software is compatible with devices running the
following operating systems: Palm OS, Windows Mobile
Pocket PC (Professional), Windows Mobile Smartphone
(Standard), Symbian Series 60 or Symbian UIQ. You can
also read Fictionwise Secure eReader eBooks on a Windows PC/Notebook, Apple Macintosh or an OQO Ultra
Portable Computer.

Fictionwise Secure **Mobipocket** titles are encrypted
eBooks that can be read with the free Mobipocket reading
software on virtually all handheld devices and on the PC.
You can download the Secure Mobipocket Reader for
Palm, Windows Mobile Pocket PC (Professional), Windows
Mobile Smartphone (Standard), BlackBerry, Symbian Se-

ries 60, 80, 90 and UIQ, WinCE, Psion, Franklin eBook-man, or PC. See
http://www.FictionWise.com

OfficeMax
http://www.ebooks.officemax.com/
MobiPocket. Now an Amazon company. MobiPocket also has versions for Palm, Pocket, PCs, and some smart phones. If you post your book at MobiPocket, it usually automatically appears at Amazon for the Kindle.
http://www.MobiPocket.com

Stanza from Lexcycle.
http://www.Stanza.com

iPhone App Store
Uses eReader or Stanza reader software
http://www.apple.com/iphone/appstore/. See Books >

For a list of eBook publishers and eBook stores, see
http://www.ebookcrossroads.com/epublishers.html

Also see Document 615, *pBooks to eBooks* at
http://DanSentMe.com/sites/para/resources/allproducts.cfm

Avoid manufacturing and shipping The CD/DVD is not the ultimate answer. To reduce costs and speed delivery, publishers should pursue digital downloads. We want to avoid manufacturing, inventory, and physical fulfillment.

Downloads can be automated, which reduces interruptions to authors and speeds delivery to our customer. Self-service is faster, easier, and cheaper.

Audiobook Distribution

Here is a short list of audiobook distributors. Like printed books, you will sell far more audios directly into the non-traditional markets.

Spoken Books Publishing, a division of Infinity Publishing. Infinity records, edits, manufactures, distributes, and sells.
http://www.spokenbookspublishing.com/

Ingram Digital
Ingram Digital sells downloads
http://www.ingramdigital.com/

Lulu.com
Lulu sells downloads
http://www.Lulu.com

Overdrive
http://www.Overdrive.com

Chapter Five

Stage Four
Promoting Your Book

Stage Four lists a myriad of ways in which to promote your book. Do those you want to do and discard those that are not fascinating to you. For example, if you enjoy gathering and disseminating information in a newsletter, publish an ezine. If you sweat deadlines and throw some text together at the last minute, don't publish an ezine. Poor newsletters only tarnish your reputation and drive you nuts.

If you are reclusive and do not wish to appear on TV, you certainly have permission not to go. But, knowing that as an author, you must promote your books, this chapter lists many other ways to fulfill your obligation to your book without getting dressed and leaving home. Promote in ways that are fun for you.

Your book will not promote itself. You have to let potential buyers know of your book. Don't abdicate your responsibility to your book.

> The biggest mistake people make when it comes to self-publishing is that that they expect to just put out a book and have it magically sell.
> — David Conroy, CNET Reviews.

Today you must be an "author-preneur."

Promoting your book is not mysterious and does not have to be expensive. Promotion simply means informing those interested in your subject that there is a book available to answer their questions and solve their problem. You can take part in web exposure, serving micro-audiences or niche markets, without leaving home.

On the other hand, if you are an extrovert looking forward to radio, TV, and autograph parties, you have to finish the book to attract the public to your events.

> The Internet and search engines such as Google help readers to find authors and their books. They also enable you to find your readers.

Authors and publishers need to engage potential readers *where they are.* An ad in the *LA Times* is very expensive and is going to a general audience. Most *Times* subscribers will not see the ad or read it. And, it doesn't interest them; it does not coincide with their lifestyle. It is more efficient and far less expensive to pursue targeted forums, blogs and other social networks as cost-effective ways to reach your specific audience.

> People no longer read the newspaper, so they no longer read or are influenced by book reviews in newspapers.
> --Michael Levin

Marketing begins before you write. It is defining your audience. That is why we recommend drafting your back-cover sales copy before writing the nonfiction book.

Promotion takes time

In book promotion, there is a long lead time and a long lag time. For example, when you send out books for review, it will take three months to three years for the reviews to appear. Keep up the pressure. As John Kremer advises: Do five things to promote your book every day—even a telephone call counts. Do not slow down and do not give up. Doing five promotional things each day will keep your book's visibility in the front of your mind.

New media is replacing old media. Newspapers are consolidating, downsizing, and going out of business. National magazines are closing bureaus, some major metro newspapers are closing down national desks, bloggers are displacing movie critics, Craigslist has replaced classified advertising, Yahoo has replaced stock quotations, and some PR reps are now specializing in social media. The handwriting is on the wall. New Media is the future and the future is now.

> "The Information Age has been superseded by the Connection Age."
> -Mike Larsen, literary agent.

Publishers have been moving book advertising money from print publications to the Web for some time; today it's becoming much more common to take a book campaign *only* online. http://www.publishersweekly.com/article/CA6559512.html

> Book publicist Stacey Miller comments: "Authors and publishers who ignore changes in the media do so at their own peril. It's not particularly enjoyable to watch newspapers' book review sections shrink or disappear altogether, and it's sad to see national and local television (not to mention radio) shows fizzle. And it's especially difficult to watch prestigious newspapers morph into something altogether new...but to deny those changes, or to hope it won't affect any other newspapers, is to jeopardize book promotion campaigns and the possibility of garnering as much book publicity opportunities now as you did in the "old days." See http://www.bookpr.com/bookpromotionblog/2008/10/kieeping_up_with_changes_to_ke.html

See *Effective Internet Presence* by Ted Demopoulos.

http://www.effectiveinternetpresence.com/articles/effecti
ve-internet-presence.pdf

Viral Marketing. Viral marketing and viral advertising
refer to marketing techniques that use pre-existing social
networks to produce increases in brand awareness or to
achieve other marketing objectives (such as product
sales) through self-replicating viral processes. It is content voluntarily passed from one person to another via
email, text messaging, via a social network posting, Facebook, Twitter, etc. The method of transmission is usually
electronic as that makes the message easy to forward.
The message may include links, images, videos, applications, games, stories, or other content.

Think about a sneeze. Several people are affected and
then they sneeze and many more pick up the virus—and
so on. That is the concept of viral marketing: getting others to spread your message—because they want to.

Viral marketing requires two things, the message and the
method. To promote books, the message is the back
cover of your book and the method is email to your own
(Outlook, etc.) list. With some luck, your message could
become viral.

Email your colleagues. Copy\Paste your back cover
sales copy and send the message to everyone in your own
address book. Do not ask your friends to buy a book, ask
them to help you. Request that they forward your book
announcement to people in their address books who
might be interested in the subject.

For example, I have a book titled *The Older Cat: Recog-
nizing Decline & Extending Life*. I sent the (back cover)
description to everyone in my Outlook address book asking my colleagues to forward the announcement to anyone in their address book with an older cat. Not to everyone, not to colleagues with a younger cat, just to those
living with a cat over ten years.

Recipients will open the email as it is from someone they know. They will be grateful for the information. They will often be motivated to re-forward the announcement. This is viral marketing and you will be reaching interested people you haven't met—yet.

Next, post your request for help at the many social media sites such as forums. Ask members to help you spread the word on your book.

These types of investments of time return huge results at zero monetary cost.

Draft a promotion checklist. Sit down and make two lists for your category of book.

1. Organizations you use, frequent or are a member of.

2. Organizations you do not use but know of.
   a. Associations and clubs
   b. Magazines and newsletters
   c. Stores
   d. Catalogs
   e. Events and conventions
   f. Forums
   g. Social networks online

Offer dealerships to most and get to know the rest (or get them to know you and your book).

The following avenues to exposure for your book, while being comfortable to the introverted writer, should be followed by all author-publishers.

Online Listings. Below is a list of sites where you can post your book cover image, blurb, and link for frèe (you may have to register with a username and password).

http://reader2.com
www.anobii.com

www.author-network.com
www.authorpromote.com
www.authorsden.com
www.authortree.com
www.babelio.com (French site)
www.bibliophil.org
www.bookhitch.com
www.booklicker.com
www.BookMesh.com
www.booksie.com
www.bookswellread.com
www.booktour.com
www.booktribes.com
www.chainreading.com
www.connectviabooks.com
www.discoverabook.com
www.editred.com
www.goodreads.com
www.gurulib.com
www.ibookdb.net
http://issuu.com/
www.jacketflap.com
www.librarything.com
www.linktiles.com
www.listal.com
www.litpitch.com
www.mediachest.com
www.nothingbinding.com
www.polkadotbanner.com
www.published.com
www.redroom.com
www.selfpublishersplace.com
www.shelfari.com
www.shelfcentered.com
www.slake.com
www.writers.net
www.writerscafe.org
www.xenite.org/internet_authors/announcebooks.html
www.zazieweb.fr (French site)

Once your book is published, you may list it frèe on the Para Publishing Website. Just click on *Success Stories* and fill in the form. Include your email address and URL so that interested surfers can click directly back to you. See http://parapublishing.com/success_list.cfm

Review copies. Review copies are the least expensive and most effective promotion you can do. The secret to getting good reviews in publications with your audience is to send review copies to *category* magazines.

For example, when Dan Poynter sends a new skydiving book to the fifty-four parachute magazines and newsletters around the world, all fifty-four review it. That is a hit rate of 100 percent! The editors like to report on new products and their readers like to find out about new products.

Sending your book to *The New York Times* is a waste of your time and money. They do not have space to mention your book and readers of the *Times* are not your audience. Large-city newspapers go to a very general audience. You want to target an interested audience.

As of this writing, there are more than ninety different categories of specific magazines. For example, there are 764 business magazines, newsletters, and newspaper columns—worldwide. There are 157 for salespeople, eighty-one for managers, fifty-four on real estate, 233 for seniors, eighty-eight for teenagers, 241 on fitness, twenty on energy and—yes—fifth-four on skydiving.

For a list of category magazines with counts, see http://parapublishing.com/sites/para/resources/maillist.cfm

Go online and make up lists of magazines, newsletters, ezines, blogs, etc. that match the subject matter of your book.

Do not email an editor asking if he or she wants to see your book. They are too busy to answer you. Get your book into their hands. Your book is its own ambassador—it speaks for itself. You can't possibly describe your book as well as it can present itself. When in doubt, ship it out.

Ship the printed book not the eBook. A physical book is easier to flip through and is more difficult to ignore.

Amazon reviewers. Amazon moves nearly 20 percent of the books in the U.S. Read about how to get your book on Amazon in the Distribution Chapter.

Below are the addresses of some of the most prolific Amazon reviewers. If your subject interests them, you have a very good chance of it being favorably reviewed on Amazon.

In addition, look up books similar to yours on Amazon. Read the reviews. Try to determine the mailing address of those reviewers who posted positive evaluations. Make Google searches for them. Send books to reviewers interested in your subject.

For more on Amazon reviewers, see
http://www.WOW-WomenOnWriting.com/17-review.html

Most Amazon reviewers have not switched to eBooks yet. Because of Amazon's Kindle, this situation may change. Meanwhile, you should send a printed book (pBook) to the group listed below. (Some addresses may no longer be correct.)

Harriet Klausner
6073 Fieldcrest Dr
Morrow, GA, 30260
HarrietKlausner@Worldnet.ATT.net

Donald Wayne Mitchell
PO Box 302
Weston, MA 02493
DonMitch@FastForward400.com

Angel Lee
Imagiart Stamps
PO Box 770913
Lakewood, OH 44107
halo@en.com

Frank Behrens
145 Concord Rd
Keene, NH 03431
Behrens@cheshire.net

Lawrance M. Bernabo, Ph.D.
Lake Superior College
814 W 5th St
Duluth, MN 55806
l.bernabo@lsc.mnscu.edu

Books-on-Line
John Matlock
242 West Railroad Street
Winnemucca, NV 89445
Review_editor@books-on-line.com

Robert Morris
10438 Pagewood Drive
Dallas, TX 75230-4254
interllect@mindspring.com

Barron Laycock
Fish Rd
Temple, NH 03084
Labradorman@hotmail.com

Roz Levine
6604 Baymeadow Ct
Mc Lean, VA 22101-1602
RozLev@cox.net

The Noh Hare
Marc Ruby
31350 Willow Ct
Warren, MI 48093-1684

Alejandra Vernon
6477 Atlantic Ave, S-324
Long Beach, CA 90805
A.Vernon@verizon.net
Http://www.aVernon.com

J. Scott Morrison
390 Blake Roy Rd
Middlebury, VT 05753-9144

Kurt A. Johnson
245 Scott St
Marseilles, IL 61341-1564
(815) 357-1224

Michael Woznicki
34 Craig Rd
Holland, MA 01521-2507
MikeW@cox.net
mikew34@cox.net

Linda Linguvic
100 Sullivan St, Apt 6C
New York, NY 10012-3629

Steve Vrana
245 Donegal Rd
Aurora, NE 68818-1434

John Kwok
PO Box 200274
Brooklyn, NY 11220

Your page on Amazon. Your book's page on Amazon can be active or passive. An active page not only lists the book, it "sells" it. It makes viewers grab their wallets in a stampede to buy it. Stress benefits. Like the back cover of your book, the book's listing page at Amazon should motivate people to buy your Work.

Amazon's description field has a limit of four thousand characters so fill the description area close to that limit. In the product description, mention previous editions and other books authored by you. If you did a great job drafting your back-cover sales copy, use again it here.

Assign an appropriate "search term" to the book to make it easy to find.

Amazon has two akin programs; one free and one paid for. "Frequently Bought Together" (sometimes seen as "Better Together") which are books chosen by Amazon to pair together and is no cost to the book publisher. Unfortunately, you have no input as to their choices.

Another program is called "Buy X Get Y" (BXGY) where you can request pairings. This advertising works best when you match your book with a top-seller in its category. Mike sure both books have the same tag.

Amazon has been known to respond to news releases so put Amazon on your book promotion mailing list.

Here are some other ways to get more exposure on Amazon. Set up an "Amazon Connect" blog on your book's page. Check into Listmania.

Success breeds success. Once the book starts selling, good things happen. "If you sell more books, you will sell more books."

Once your title is listed with Amazon, you can update the description, add a graphic image, or post reviews on the books listing page. To make changes, display your e-book listing on Amazon.com and look just below where the graphic image is displayed (or should be displayed if you don't have one). You should find a link that says Publishers: Learn how customers can search inside this book. Click on the link, type in your Amazon login information, and you will be taken to list of choices for updating the contents of your books page. Amazon will typically update the changes you submit within a week.

> With most major magazines and newspapers cutting their book sections, book reviews are moving back into the hands of the people—the readers, not the critics.
> — Annette Fix

Online Review Sites

http://www.SelfPublishingReview.com/
See the list of online review sites at
http://www.WOW-WomenOnWriting.com/17-review.html

Articles. Each thirty days after you send out the review copies, send articles to many of the same category magazines.

Just take a page from your book, add a headline, introductory paragraph, closing paragraph, and ordering instructions.

As a published author, you are a prestige contributor to magazines in your field. Editors want your material as part of their content. The value of the content is what they sell to their readership.

Always sign your submissions, "Extracted from (title of book), copyright © 2009, John Doe, www.yoursite.com"

If a magazine has a large circulation, you may even be paid for the article. But mostly, you want the credibility and exposure that goes with publication of the article.

Once the article appears, place the piece in an Article Bank on your website for other periodicals. For article outlines and an example of an Article Bank, see
http://parapublishing.com/sites/para/resources/articlebank.cfm

Contribute to articles. As a published author, you are a celebrity and an authority. You can find and help (article) writers and editors looking for information resources by subscribing to the following services.

http://www.PRNewswire.com
http://www.ProfNet.com
http://www.HelpAReporter.com

Sign up. You will be notified when a reporter is working on an article covering your subject area.

News Releases. Traditionally, news releases are never longer than four hundred words, and fit on a single 8.5"x11" page. The object of a news release is to spark interest so the reporter or editor will get back to you for an article on you and your book.

The headline is crucial, since studies show that editors often decide whether to pursue a story within *three seconds* of receiving a release.

News releases no longer have to be just printed pages. Now releases can contain video clips, hot links to other pages, images, audio files, and feedback mechanisms for readers. Always include a picture of the front cover of your book in the release. Enhance your releases.

Here are some online media distribution services:
http://www.Businesswire.com
http://www.PRNewswire.com
http://www.PRweb.com

Paul Krupin at http://www.directcontactpr.com offers news release consulting and distribution.

For more information on how to draft news releases, see *News Releases and Book Publicity at* http://DanSentMe.com/sites/para/resources/allproducts.cfm

News releases should be posted on your website in a "Newsroom" or "Pressroom"—a separate web page—after you send them to the media. Let other periodicals use them.

On-air interviews. If you like doing radio and TV, a book is your entrée. Most of the people being interviewed are authors with a new book.

Radio-TV Interview Report can get you on the show. The rest is up to you. If you are interesting and make your subject fascinating, you will sell more books than an interviewee who is dull.
http://www.RTIR.com

Select your audience.
For example, Alex Carroll uses radio exclusively to promote his book. He selects 50,000-watt stations and interviews in *drive-time* only. He is very busy early in the morning and late in the afternoon. He sells enough books to be able to afford to live in Santa Barbara.
How?
He is a great interview and his book is titled *How to Beat Your Traffic Ticket.*
Look for radio programs serving *your* audience.

If you are a reclusive author who finds that radio interviews only make you anxious, don't bother with interviews. You probably will not be good enough at them to sell many books. On the other hand, if you are an extrovert, if you love your subject and your audience, you will probably be very successful with radio.

Eventually, you will work your way up to television—and then to the bigger shows.

The six most important words in book promotion:
Nice to see you *again,* Oprah!

For more information on how to get on TV and radio shows, see Document 602 on our website.
http://parapub.com/sites/para/resources/allproducts.cfm

Need someone to get you on radio and TV? See the Supplier List at:
http://parapub.com/sites/para/resources/supplier.cfm

Want radio and TV coaching? See the Supplier List at:
http://parapub.com/sites/para/resources/supplier.cfm

Blog talk radio. Launched in 2006, Blog Talk Radio attracts nearly two million listeners a month. The system allows users to field phone calls, upload music, and effectively run a live radio show that can be archived. The free service makes its money by selling advertising.
http://www.blogtalkradio.com/

Your website. Of course, you need a website. You need a destination to drive the eyeballs to. Establish a firm online presence.

Your website is your brochure—without the printing and mailing costs. It is also your storefront and the store is open to the world twenty-four hours a day.

The Web is a direct-response medium. Responses are trackable. You can determine who is responding to your posts.

Websites should be rich in content; they should sell content with content. Post information from your book in order to sell the entire book.

Many Internet-marketing experts recommend setting up a one-page website for your book. It can also be linked to your master website. The single-topic website will be picked up by search engines.

Answer your email. Many introverted writers want to concentrate on book creation and do not want to correspond with their adoring readers.

As a published author you have both an obligation and an opportunity. Readers paid money for your book and you owe them answers to their questions. Responding to their email queries also provides you with feedback on your book and a way to find out what more they want to know.

They may also find errors. This information can be used in revised editions and new books. Direct them to your book's information page on your website.

Information kit. A free InfoKit on your subject helps people on their schedule, trims back on interrupting telephone inquiries, makes you appear to be generous, builds your house mailing list, and provides more traffic to your website.

We now have three InfoKits, and each is more than twenty pages of targeted information. There is one on book writing, one on production, and a third on promotion. Our server fulfills nearly a thousand requests each month—automatically.

Collect your emailed questions and the answers and put them into an InfoKit. Refresh it with new information periodically; let it grow. Then begin splitting it.

Email signature. Having a signature (.sig) at the end of your emails will drive eyeballs back to your website.

A signature tells recipients of your messages, who you are, what you do, and how to reach you. It drives attention back to your website.

Here is an example of an email signature.

Speaking in Singapore, Sydney next. When I am traveling, my messages and answers tend be short. Thank you for your understanding.
~~~~~~

Dan Poynter, Author (120+ books), Publisher (since 1969), Speaker (CSP).
Para Publishing, PO Box 8206, Santa Barbara, CA 93118-8206 USA.
Bus: +1-805-968-7277, Mob: +1-805-448-9009.
DanPoynter@ParaPublishing.com,
http://ParaPublishing.com
NOW, SIT DOWN AND WRITE SOMETHING.

If you are using an email program such as Outlook or AOL, click on Help and type in Signature. A box will pop up telling how to craft one. It may take you ten minutes the first time. Later changes may take a minute.

Besides your email signature, you should also have a matching business card.

Book trailers—video promotion. YouTube is growing in popularity and deserves serious attention. Even if you can only afford to get a bare bones author interview video-taped and uploaded, it's a good investment.

http://www,YouTube.com
http://www.AuthorBytes.com
http://www.PromoteABookStudios.com

On the other hand, your potential buyers are book read-ers. Readers are print-oriented. Promoting your book to them via video will not be as effective as print promotion. The best way to promote print is with print. So get some-thing up on sites such as YouTube but do not spend too much time doing it.
http://www.youtube.com/watch?v=9kJr59Xcf30

Social media—social networking. Sharing your thoughts, information, and ideas with people around the world interested in your subject can easily be done through "social media." Via the Internet, others can find you and you can find them. This is birds of a feather flocking together; "hanging out" with your (new) friends.

Social networking is not new; it has been around since the camp-fire. The only difference is that today, the birds are flocking to-gether online and with mobile phones. These are new ways that offer new places to flock.

Only the technology has changed. For example, from smoke signals to homing pigeons to mobile phone text messaging, the new ways are just faster, easier, and cheaper. Besides, mobile phones eat less than pigeons and are not as messy as pigeons.

> "For all the hype about social networking websites, the most popular and successful way to market over the Internet is still the oldest: email."
> —Walter S. Mossberg, *The Wall Street Journal.*

Google defines social networking as linking people to each other in some way.

Wikipedia says social media can take many different forms, including Internet forums, message boards, weblogs, wikis, podcasts, pictures, and video. Technologies include: blogs, picture-sharing, vlogs, wall-postings, email, instant messaging, music-sharing, crowdsourcing, and voice over IP, to name a few.

Examples of social media applications are Google Groups (reference, social networking), Wikipedia (reference), MySpace (social networking), Facebook (social networking), Last.fm (personal music), YouTube (social networking and video sharing), Second Life (virtual reality), Flickr (photo sharing), Twitter (social networking and microblogging). Other microblogs are Jaiku and Pownce. Many of these social media services can be integrated via social network aggregation platforms like Mybloglog and Plaxo. See
http://en.wikipedia.org/wiki/Social_media

What does this mean?
Simply, this is people sharing information and ideas with others who have a common interest. As authors and publishers of nonfiction, we are in the information business. The Internet makes it possible to find and interact with colleagues—all over the world. Birds of a feather are indeed flocking together.

From now on many books will evolve from static, printed pages to an optimized web presence incorporating inter-activity, sharing, and collaboration. See http://www.newcommreview.com/?p=944

Using social networking sites isn't so much about solicit-ing business as it is about establishing yourself as a real, live person with whom others may wish to do business.

Social networking for *authors*. Social networking can get publicity for your book and develop a following for the book. As a nonfiction author, you are in the information business. You are an AUTHOR-ity, an expert, a resource. People interested in your subject want to find you and "hang out" with you.

As we've discussed, there are many types of social networking communications such as text messaging, voice chat, etc. We will concentrate on the networking that is being used to promote books.

If you're an **extroverted** verbal person, you may reach your target audience through audio books, podcasts, ra-dio, TV, and other **verbal** delivery.

If you're **introverted** writer, you may reach your target audience through magazine articles, email, and taking part in online forums. In other words: **written** delivery.

The question is would you rather type or talk? Are you an author or a professional speaker?

Discussion groups. Forums or listservs are places on the Web for discussing specific issues. The postings usually come to you via email.

Since some of the members of the forum have been around a long time and are quite knowledgeable, you can get a lot of free consulting by joining. Forums can be used to gather information as well as to publicize your books.

In book publishing, there are four general forums and several specific ones. The general ones are:

Pub-Forum
http://www.pub-forum.net/

Self-Publishing
http://finance.groups.yahoo.com/group/self-publishing/

PUBLISH-L
http://www.publish-l.com/

SmallPubCivil
http://finance.groups.yahoo.com/group/smallpub-civil/

Other forums for specialized topics in publishing include:

Fiction_L.
http://www.webrary.org/rs/flmenu.html

Children's Books
http://www.egroups.com/search?query=youngchildrensbooks

Children's Books
http://groups.yahoo.com/group/CBpublishing/

IND-E-PUBS. eBooks
http://www.ind-e-pubs.com/
http://groups.yahoo.com/group/ebook-community/

POD Publishers
http://finance.groups.yahoo.com/group/pod_publishers/

Publishing Design
http://groups.yahoo.com/group/publishingdesign/

Book Signings/Mini seminars
http://groups.yahoo.com/group/booksigners/

Copy Law
http://groups.yahoo.com/group/copyright-future

Category forums. Go to http://www.groups.yahoo.com to look for forums that concentrate on your book's genre.

Freely interact with published authors, writers, poets, readers, and publishing professionals by going to http://www.authornation.com. There's no charge and this unique website is completely free of commercial advertising. Post your Work-in-progress to be critiqued, ask for suggestions, promote your Work, and seek free advice from industry pros.

Draw attention to your book with a quiz. Discover what your potential readers are thinking and what they want to read while drawing their attention to your Work. Take and create online quizzes and then share the results with colleagues.
http://www.quibblo.com/

This is a free service that allows anyone to set up online polls, surveys, or quizzes pertaining to a topic of their choice.

Forums/social networks for book *readers.* There are social networks for book readers that allow members to look at other members' bookshelves for the purpose of spotting new titles read by people with similar interests. These are online reading groups. Some sites have a book-selling function. See

http://www.Shelfari.com
http://www.BookMesh.com

http://www.BookRabbit.com
http://www.GoodReads.com
http://www.amazon.com/gp/help/customer/display.html?
nodeId=468600
http://www.BookJetty.com

Blogs. Blogs or "weblogs" are usually hosted by one person and contain his or her written observations, thoughts, and even rants. Most invite comment in order to spark a discussion.

In a blog, authors can lead/monitor/incite discussions and try to build a following.

Some authors are using blogs very effectively to build communities around the subject matter of their books. On the other hand, some people observe there are more bloggers than readers. Who can read it all?

Don't feel obligated to start another blog. Do it only if blogging has a strong appeal to you.

You can syndicate your blog to social networking sites such as Facebook and Plaxo. Syndication will increase your circulation.

Contribute to blogs in your book's subject area. Always sign your (generous and positive) postings with your name, book title, and website URL. With your content, drive attention to your website and buyers toward your book.

Give bloggers a scoop. Publicist Joan Stewart suggests: If you write and distribute press releases online, you're in an ideal position to give bloggers a scoop.

Before you distribute the release, simply email your favorite blogger with a "heads up" that you'll be posting the release later that day. Explain the essence of the release, or just give it to them. See http://publicityhound.net

Blogs on book publishing
http://indieKindle.blogspot.com/
http://thekindle.wordpress.com/2008/12/20/the-kindle-blogs-book-publishing/

To find more blogs, do a Google search for "Blog + Books" and "Blog + (your subject)."

Blog platforms. For tools for blogging, see
http://www.WordPress.org
http://www.Blogger.com
http://www.Typepad.com
http://www.Tumblr.com
http://posterous.com/

Blog submission sites. To find blog submission sites, see
http://www.technorati.com
http://www.google.com/blogsearch
http://www.BlogPulse.com

XML feed file software. RSS (Really Simple Syndication) is the standard for content distribution and syndication. With feed file software, you can create, edit, and publish RSS feeds. See
http://www.FeedForAll.com
http://www.FeedBurner.com

Blogcasting. A blogcast is the combination of a blog and podcast into a single website. A blogcast enables you to create both. With a blogcast, you can freely add text, photos, and music to your blogcast entries.

Web-based feed aggregators. For a list, see
http://www.NewsOnFeeds.com/faq/aggregators

Podcasting. Podcasting is *audio* blogging. The blogger speaks rather than types. For submission sites, see

http://www.apple.com/itunes/store/podcasts.html
http://www.AudioAcrobat.com
http://www.odeo.com
http://www.podcast.com
http://www.PRwebPodcast.com
http://www.WordPress.org
http://www.authorbytes.com/

Video podcast. Vidcasts or vodcasts are used for the online delivery of video-on-demand and video clip content via Atom or RSS enclosures. For submission sites, see
http://www.vlog.tv
http://www.vlogmap.org

Webcasting. Webcasting is broadcasting over the Internet. A webinar (web seminar) is an example. These are media files distributed over the Internet using streaming media technology. A webcast may either be distributed live or recorded.

> People are using Wikipedia, and you should be using it, too, whatever your feelings about a democratic ency-clopedia that allows anyone, regardless of credentials, to offer suggestions. It's easy to enter your own bio in Wikipedia and, hopefully, score a backlink to your Website and your fair share of Google's attention. Yes, it's an offbeat book promotion idea, but it's one that authors and publishers should be using, anyway. Try it, and don't be shy—it's impossible to "break" Wikipedia or your own entry. I promise. You can always edit your offering once you've uploaded it to Wikipedia to test it out "live."
> —Stacey Miller, publicist

Wikis. Wikis (Hawaiian meaning *fast*) are collaborative websites allowing people to update the information from their personal experience and research. The listings be-come an ever-evolving database of information. Wikis could replace many types of nonfiction books just as has happened with printed encyclopedias. See

http://www.Wikipedia.com
http://www.WikiDot.com
http://www.MediaWiki.org

Written, audio, or video? Written blogs can be quickly scanned for interesting items. Verbal podcasting is linear and must be listened to or watched in sequence. People may not spend the time to find if there is anything that could interest them.

Infotainment. You must be *very* entertaining to get people to listen to or watch you.

Submission sites. Once you have a blog, podcast, vidcast, or any RSS feed, you should take advantage of some submission sites.

Just go to each site and follow the feed submission guidelines at each one. Many of them will also allow you to add descriptions, keywords, or "tags" for your feed. They will help people interested in your subject to find you.

For more information see the explanations, examples, and resources at
http://www.pma-online.org/articles/shownews.aspx?id=2565

Virtual book tours. Authors have choices when booking book tours; you don't need to travel long distances or worry about the travel arrangements and expenses. Many authors are choosing to promote their book with a virtual tour. A virtual book tour is exactly what it says—a book tour that you can conduct entirely from the privacy of your home or office!
http://www.bloomingtwigbooks.com/blog/2008/06/09/virtual-book-tours/

Social bookmarking. Websites where users create and store Internet bookmarks. These bookmarks can be viewed by others, letting them know about new services

and the latest concepts making news in the online world.
See
http://del.icio.us
http://www.faves.com
http://www.ma.gnolia.com
http://www.stumbleupon.com
http://www.technorati.com

For more, see the lists at:
http://www.en.wikipedia.org/wiki/List_of_social_software #Social_bookmarking
http://www.maxpower.ca/bookmarking
http://www.squidoo.com/socialbookmarkingsites

Social networking sites/services. Help people with your interests to find you and your book. Popular social networking services now allow you to combine many ways to communicate: text, audio, video, and photographs.

Explore the listed sites to find out which ones fit you best. Check with colleagues in your interest area or industry to find which services they favor. Below are some options to get you started.

a. Business-oriented networking sites

LinkedIn offers an opportunity to network with other professionals from a diversity of backgrounds.
http://www.Linked-In.com
Also see
http://www.ryze.com
http://SelfGrowth.com

b. More social-networking sites
Facebook is made up of many networks—join one or create your own. It is said that your pages on Facebook will result in higher search-engine rankings for your website.
http://www.FaceBook.com

Myspace is a popular networking site for teens that offers complete profile options with various groups.
http://www.MySpace.com

Bebo is popular in Europe.
http://www.Bebo.com

Plaxo
http://www.Plaxo.com

In the short time I've been on Twitter, I've seen amaz-
ing things happen: a speaking gig, a strong lead on a
copywriting client, a whole lot of new and very valuable
contacts, a ton of resources I'd have missed...and of
course, deepening personal connections. But you have
to be strategic with it. I post content that positions me
as helpful, knowledgeable and friendly/accessible—and
with outside interests besides making bucks.
— Shel Horowitz,
http://principledprofit.com/good-business-blog/loving-
twitter/2008/12/20/

Twitter, it turns out, is attracting the attention of many
journalists and broadcasters who are actually using it
to look for sources for their stories and guests for their
shows. For patient Publicity Hounds on Twitter, that
means big-time media hits in traditional media outlets
if you're following these journalists and you can provide what they need. You can find a list of journalists
who Twitter at
http://my-creativeteam.com/blog/?p=694
— Joan Stewart, The Publicity Hound.
http://www.ThePublicityHound.com

Twitter is a service in which people follow each other's
day-to-day activities in short text messages (up to 140
characters). You can tell your "followers" what you are
doing—such as bringing out a new book. They may pass

the announcement on to their followers. The posts are archived and can be found with search engines.

http://www.Twitter.com
http://www.youtube.com/watch?v=IUR2E8l3bi8
http://www.my-creativeteam.com/blog/?p=821
http://www.PublicityHound.com/publicity-products/marketing-tapes/twitter.htm
To find out what reporters are working on, "follow" them at:
http://www.search.twitter.com

All of these social networks are evolving. What I have described so far is accurate. By tomorrow, some of it could be completely obsolete.

You can even start your own social network! You can create your own network and establish yourself as an expert. Ning.com <http://www.ning.com> is a free online service that allows you to create, customize, and share your own social network. You can choose your own combination of features for your site, from videos to blogs to forums, and even add your own brand logo. Start up a network relevant to the content of your book and watch your platform grow.

I am not necessarily recommending you do this. My purpose here is to show you how to take advantage of the *existing* networks.

Once you get into posting on blogs, forums, etc, you will learn and find ways to expand your participation.

> According to eContentMag.com, workers in the UK spend at least thirty minutes each day visiting social networking sites. This personal surfing costs businesses $13 billion annually.

Millions of people are engaged in social networking—they are seeking your message.

Social networking **will sell** more books.

> I have always been a social networker and I sus-
> pect that most of you have been too. My initial
> books were on parachutes and hang gliding. As a
> pilot and a skydiver, I hung around with fellow
> aviators.
>
> It was 1977 when I went to my first book fair in
> Los Angeles and suddenly discovered that I was a
> publisher. I thought I was just a member of the
> parachute industry and a member of the hang glid-
> ing industry who enjoyed writing about my avia-
> tion passions.
> — Dan Poynter

RSS feed submission sites and feed services. RSS
(Really Simple Syndication) are Web feed formats used
to publish frequently updated content such as blog
entries, news headlines, and podcasts in a
standardized format.

An RSS document (which is called a "feed" or "web feed"
or "channel") contains either a summary of content from
an associated website or the full text. An RSS feed allows
you to place information on your site and offer it to
subscribers.

See an example author interview at
http://www.InsideScoopLive.com

Amazon RSS feeds
http://www.amazon.com/gp/help/customer/display.html?i
e=UTF8&nodeId=200202840

RSS feed services.
 http://www.avangate.com/articles/rss-submission-
directories_58.htm
http://www.FeedBurner.com
http://www.RSSpad.com

http://www.press-feed.com/howitworks/howpromotefeeds.php
http://www.rssfeeds.com/links.php
http://www.rss-specifications.com/rss-submission.htm
http://www.DummySoftware.com/RSSsubmit.html

Media communities. A media community is a place where you can upload and share images (photos), audio files, video, and so on. Make sure you mention your web-site in order to lure people's attention back to it. Here are some examples:

http://www.betyourboots.com/photo.html
http://www.en.wikipedia.org/wiki/Photo_sharing
http://www.en.wikipedia.org/wiki/List_of_video_sharing_websites

Media sharing. Media communities are places where you can upload your photos and videos. Posting photos and videos can drive surfers to your website.

Tag your uploads with numerous and accurate keywords so that people interested in your subject will find the postings (and you).

Image-sharing communities. Post photos of your book covers and yourself.

http://www.comboost.com
http://www.Flickr.com
http://www.gallery.menalto.com
http://www.picasa.google.com/
http://www.myalbum.com
http://www.photobucket.com

Video-sharing communities. Post book trailers.
http://www.buzznet.com/video
http://www.metacafe.com
http://www.video.google.com
http://www.YouTube.com

Webcasting. Webcasting allows you to broadcast images, audio, video, text, etc.
http://www.bliptv.com
http://www.bogtv.com
http://www.SplashCastMedia.com
http://www.YouTube.com

Widgets/Badges. These are computer codes that can be added to a blog, web page, or social networking page to increase its interactivity. Widgets have been around since 2001 but are now a hot Web 2.0 tool. Examples are Google's Book Bar Wizard, Twitter Widget, and The Flickr Slideshow.
http://www.WidgetBox.com
http://www.Directory.Snipperoo.com
http://www.code.google.com/apis/OpenSocial

Blidgets. A small widget for feeding blog posts to other sites.
http://www.WidgetBox.com

Mashups. Fancy widgets.
http://www.GoogleMashups.com
http://www.pipes.yahoo.com
http://www.ProgammableWeb.com

TweetBeep. "Google Alert" for Twitter
http://www.TweetBeep.com

Times (and technology) change. Changes in the Internet, new media and other exciting developments favor the more nimble small publisher. Web 2.0 and social media are spawning author-controlled publishing.

In the early 1990s, I gathered up all my fancy camera equipment and took it to the camera store to sell. I made a vow not to buy any camera or other electronic equipment that was not digital. That vow has paid off.

We authors and publishers took advantage of new technology earlier than people in most fields. Many of us purchased our computers in the early to mid-1980s. Our rationale was that as craftspeople we deserve the very best tools. Then we discovered that the computer was good for more than writing. We could also use it for research, typesetting and for book promotion.

So social networking isn't so scary, is it? You're simply dealing with the people you feel most comfortable with—your friends. Reaching other people who like to discuss your favorite subjects is not intimidating, it's fun. Technology, the Internet, and e-mail, make social networking faster, easier, and cheaper. Birds of a feather flock together.

The future (measured in weeks) ☺
Book publishing is changing. Soon the author will be closer to the reader. All the middle people will be cut out of the income stream.

Authors will be able to sell their books (pBooks, eBooks, etc) for less because they will not be sharing the income with agents, publishers, wholesalers, bookstores, distributors, and the rest of the gatekeepers in the middle.

The computer and the Internet make streamlining possible. Authors are able to find willing buyers and readers are able to find authors by using the search engines for research.

The author's personal websites will deliver the entertainment (fiction) or information (nonfiction) automatically.

Many books will evolve from static, printed pages to an optimized web presence incorporating interactivity, sharing, and collaboration. Visit
http://www.newcommreview.com/?p=944

In the (near) future, it is likely books will be posted online. Frēe books will be supported by Google Ads. If there is a large amount of interest, the book will be committed to ink and paper—but the information will be old, at least a month old. In effect, the publication cycle will be reversed.

Some nonfiction will be networked wikis by subject. Books will be read and grow in a network context. Remember, Wikipedia grew from encyclopedias. People all over the world will be adding to and benefiting from the content. Many people will contribute their experiences to the "book" or file. They will grow and be up-to-date. Think Web 2.0/3.0.

We will always have printed books, but they will be fiction, coffee table books (Works of art), and nonfiction that is so popular it has earned a print run.

Welcome to the new world of book publishing.

Appendix

Your Book's Calendar

The following checklist describes what do to at each stage of your book.

One of the largest pitfalls in small publishing is the lack of sufficient planning, especially the first time around. You don't want to tie up funds by purchasing materials and services too soon and you don't want to miss some important publicity because you missed a filing date.

This checklist will help keep you on track. Follow this schedule for your first book. On your second book, you will want to move some items up, and skip some others.

References may be made to The Self-Publishing Manual, Volume One (SPM-1) or The Self-Publishing Manual, Volume 2 (SPM-2).

Some referenced forms and applications are available from the Para Publishing website. Documents numbered 1xx or 6xx are available from http://DanSentMe.com/sites/para/resources/allproducts.cfm

1. Now—things you should do right now:

  Get the InfoKit on book writing at http://parapublishing.com/sites/para/resources/infokit.cfm
  Join the Publishers Marketing Association (IBPA). http://www.PMAonline.org. See the newsletter and get a membership application. One co-op marketing program will pay for your membership.
  Get copyright forms from the Library of Congress. http://www.copyright.gov/forms/
Get Document 112 (frèe) from http://DanSentMe.com/sites/para/resources/allproducts.cfm
  See *Publishers Weekly* at http://www.publishersweekly.com/eNewsletterArchive/2286.html

☐ Choose a company name. File a fictitious name statement, if required. See Chapter 3 in *The Self-Publishing Manual, Volume I*.

☐ Purchase some office supplies. See Chapter 3 in *SPM, Volume I*

☐ Get ABI Information. See page 88

☐ Apply for a post office box. See Chapter 3, *SPM, Vol. I*.

☐ Read the latest edition of *The Self Publishing Manual*, *Volume I* completely and highlight important areas.

☐ Contact the Small Business Administration about its services. Call your local office. See Chapter 3, *SPM, Vol. I*.

☐ Apply for any local business licenses. Ask other nearby small businesspeople for advice. Do not call the city licensing offices for information. See Chapter 3, *SPM, Vol. I*

☐ Draft your book's back-cover sales copy. See Chapter 2 *SPM, Vol. I* and get Document 116 (frèe) at http://DanSentMe.com/sites/para/resources/allproducts.cfm

☐ Get *Writing Nonfiction: turning thoughts into books*. See http://ParaPublishing.com.

☐ Add a signature to your email program. See pages 66 and 119

2. While writing your book:

☐ Review Chapter 2 in *SPM, Vol. I*.

☐ Get ISBN/SAN information. Page 86

☐ Solicit stories for your manuscript. Page 44.

☐ Get *The Book Publishing Encyclopedia: Tips & Resources for Authors & Publishers*. See http://DanSentMe.com/sites/para/resources/allproducts.cfm

☐ Engage an editor. Many are booked months in advance. See http://www.parapublishing.com/sites/para/resources/supplier.cfm

☐ If using a book designer or typesetter, engage that person now for the same reason. See http://www.parapublishing.com/sites/para/resources/supplier.cfm

3. When your manuscript is nearly complete:

☐ Get the InfoKit on book publishing at http://parapublishing.com/sites/para/resources/infokit.cfm

☐ Send requests for quotation to the twenty-plus digital and/or the forty-plus offset printers. Page 53. See Document 603 at http://DanSentMe.com/sites/para/resources/allproducts.cfm

☐ Purchase a set of ISBNs from R.R. Bowker. See Chapter 5 and Document 112 (frèe).

☐ Hire a cover designer to produce the book's cover. See http://parapublishing.com/sites/para/resources/supplier.cfm

☐ Fill out the ABI form. Page 88.

☐ See the Library of Congress for your LCCC number. Page 88 and Document 112 (frèe) at http://DanSentMe.com/sites/para/resources/allproducts.cfm

☐ Research your title to make sure it is not being used. See an online

bookstore such as Amazon.com and make a Google search.
- Get any needed permissions from people pictured or quoted in the book.
- Send your manuscript out for peer review (content feedback) and editing. Page 46
- Solicit testimonials. See *Blurbs for Your Books*, Document 609, at http://DanSentMe.com/sites/para/resources/allproducts.cfm

4. When the typesetter has completed your manuscript layout:

- Assign the ISBN(s). Page 86. See Chapter 5 of *SPM, Vol. I.*
- Prepare a news release. Page 116.
- Contact book clubs. See Chapter 8 in *SPM-1.*
- Apply for a resale permit. See Chapter 3 in *SPM-1.*

5. While the book is being typeset:

- Get the InfoKit on book promoting at http://parapublishing.com/sites/para/resources/infokit.cfm
- Set up storage and shipping areas. See Chapter 10 of *SPM, Vol. I.*
- Get the Special Report *Book Fulfillment, Order Entry, Picking, Packing, and Shipping* at http://parapub.com/getpage.cfm?file=products.html.
- If you are subcontracting the typesetting, maintain a good proofreading schedule. Don't hold up your typesetter.
- If you have an index, it must be done at the same time as the proofreading, so the index numbers match.
- Prepare mailing lists. See Chapter 9 in *SPM, Vol. I.*
- Order shipping supplies and the rest of your office supplies. See *SPM-1*, Chapter 10.
- Send a book announcement to all wholesalers. See our Special Report *Book Marketing*. http://parapub.com/getpage.cfm?file=products.html.
- Prepare your prepublication offer. See Chapter 8 of *SPM, Vol. I.*
- Print out book review slips and order rubber stamps. See *SPM-1*, Chapter 7.
- Pursue subsidiary rights. See *SPM-1*, Chapter 8 and the Special Report *Book Marketing*.
- Send for Special Reports *Book Marketing: A New Approach, Book Reviews, News Releases, and Book Publicity* and *Export/Foreign Rights.*
- Develop your marketing plan using the *Book Marketing* Special Report. Also see *Best Sellers*, Document 612.
- Order bar code or make sure your cover artist is taking care of it.
- Select a book printer. See Special Report *Buying Book Printing* or see Document 603. For most books, the initial print run should be around five hundred copies. You need a quantity of books to send for review, to opinion-molders in your field, and to those who helped you with peer reviewing, stories, etc. See the printing chapter of *SPM, Vol. I.*
- Order business cards with a photo of the book's cover. See *SPM-1*,

Chapter seven.

6. While the book is being printed:

📖 Proof press proofs carefully. See Special Report *Book Production.*
📖 Prepare review copy materials. Stuff and label the shipping bags, then put them aside until the books arrive.
📖 Add book information to your website or update the description.
📖 Email your prepublication offer to individuals on your mailing list.
📖 Change the signature in your email program. Mention your new book. See pages 66 and 119.
📖 List your book with Para Publishing's *Success Stories*. See http://parapublishing.com/sites/para/resources/successstories.cfm

7. When the printed books arrive:

📖 Check the quality of the books. Make a count for your inventory. See Special Report *Book Fulfillment.*
📖 Fill orders.
📖 Scan the cover of the book. Add 72 dpi jpg and 300 dpi tif to your picture file.
📖 Pursue dealer sales.
📖 File copyright form CO. See pages 42, 44 and Chapter 5 of *SPM, Vol. I.*
📖 Send books to reviewers. Page 110. See Chapter 7 of *SPM, Vol. I.*
📖 Pursue promotional possibilities in Chapter 7 of *SPM, Vol. I*, and see *Best Sellers*, Document 612. http://DanSentMe.com/sites/para/resources/allproducts.cfm
📖 Visit bookstores in your area.
📖 Submit request to *Publishing Poynters Marketplace* for reviews in Amazon.com, B&N.com, and other online bookseller sites. See http://parapublishing.com/sites/para/resources/newsletter.cfm
📖 Convert pages of your book into articles and send them to category magazines. Page 115.
📖 Email your back-cover sales copy to everyone in your address book. Ask them to forward the announcement to their colleagues. See Page 107 and Chapter 7 in *SPM-1.*
📖 Send finished copies of the book to selected agents and publishers. Give them a chance to bid on it. See page 24 and Chapter 1 of *SPM, Vol. I.*
📖 Announce your book by posting requests for help to social media sites. See pages 119, 129.

8. Ongoing promotion:

Never give up. You have given birth to your book; now you have an obligation to raise it. Review what has worked and do more of it. Review what has not worked and cut your losses.

🕮 Pursue consumer-oriented promotions such as book launches, autograph parties, talk shows, author tours, etc. See Chapter 7 in *SPM, Vol. I*, and *Interviews: How Authors Get on Radio and TV*, Document 602.
🕮 Work on nontraditional or special sales. See page 99.
🕮 Implement your continuing review program.
🕮 Consider more direct email solicitations.
🕮 Look for spin-off ideas. Repackage your information: audiobooks, electronic books, large PRINT books, etc. Consider consulting in your area of expertise. See Document 615.
🕮 Make up a review/testimonial sheet. Paste up good reviews and reproduce them. See Chapter 7 in *SPM Vol. I*.

Colophon

This book was completely produced using the New Model production system described within.

Writing and manuscript building
Manuscript preparation: MS Word
Type
  Body text: Verdana, 10, 11 pt.
  Headers: Verdana, 11, 12 pt.
  Chapter titles: Verdana, 14, 20 pt.
  Lists: Verdana, 8 pt.

Prepress
Copyediting: PenUltimate Editorial Services, Arlene Prunkl
http://www.penultimateword.com

Cover design
Robert Howard, RH Graphic Design.
http://www.BookGraphics.com

File conversion
MS Word to PDF with Adobe Acrobat 9.0

Printing
Printing by McNaughton & Gunn, Ann Arbor, Michigan
http://www.bookprinters.com from PDF file.
Paper: 60# white offset book
Cover: 10 pt C1S, four color, layflat film lamination.
Binding: Perfect bound (adhesive, softcover)

Index

If you are reading the eBook edition of this book, also use the Search feature to find the items you seek.

"I've never met an author that was sorry he or she wrote their book. They are only sorry they did not write it sooner."

— Sam Horn, Author & Speaker

QUICK ORDER FORM

Satisfaction guaranteed

▣ **email orders**: Orders@ParaPublishing.com

▤ **Fax orders:** +1-805-968-1379. Send this form.

☎ **Telephone orders:** Call +1-805-968-7277
Have your credit card ready.

▤ **Postal orders:** PO Box 8206, Santa Barbara, CA 93118-8206
USA

Please send the following Books, CDs, or Courses.
I understand that I may return any of them for a full refund—for
any reason, no questions asked.

See our website for frèe information on other books, Speak-
ing/Seminars, Mailing lists, Consulting.

Name:

Address:

City, State/Province, Postal Code:

Tel:

Email:

Payment: Check: Credit card:
    Visa   MasterCard   Optima   AMEX   Discover

Card number:

Name on card:

Exp. date: (mm/yy)